THE GNOSTIC

VOLUME FIVE

ON THE SECRET TEACHINGS AND THE HIDDEN MYTHOS

by
Timothy James Lambert

Table of Contents

<u>Introduction</u>

This book is the culmination of a project I began in the second volume of this series. In that book, I revealed a list from an apocryphal text known as the Secret Book of James. The document claimed if one truly understood the seven canonical parables on this list then that person would come to know the secret teaching of Jesus.

This search explored four of the seven parables in Volume Two. Volume Three unlocked the significance of two more parables. Volume Four was a continuation of Volume Three's exploration of Biblical Genesis. Where Volume Three focused on the first creation story from Genesis, Volume Four began with an examination of the second. This was necessary to reveal more of the systemic foundation of the background system. Finally, in the present volume, all of the strands are ready to be woven together and the final parable unveiled.

The best way to approach this book is to have read all of the previous volumes in order. If that is not possible, then one should have at least read the previous book. Then again I sometimes wonder if reading the entire series in reverse order might not reveal hidden facets of meaning concealed beneath the various layers.

The Secret Teachings of Jesus

Those of you who have been reading this series from its beginning will remember that in the second book I cited a section from the Secret Book of James:

"Since I have already been glorified in this fashion, why do you hold me back in my eagerness to go? For after the labor, you have compelled me to stay with you another eighteen days for the sake of the parables. It was enough for some <to listen> to the teaching and understand 'The Shepherds' and 'The Seed' and 'The Building' and 'The Lamps of the Virgins' and 'The Wage of the Workmen' and the 'Coins' and 'The Woman.'"
(ApoJ 4:13-15)

The remainder of the second book dealt with the parables 'The Shepherds', 'The Seed,' 'The Building', and the 'Coins.' An entirely new book, the third in the series, was required to explain the next two parables 'The Lamps of the Virgins' and 'The Wage of the Workmen.' Then in the fourth book, I went ahead and continued with the examination of Genesis begun in the third. That brings us to the present book, Volume Five in the Gnostic Notebook series. There is only a single parable left: 'The Woman.' Once we determine this parable's hidden meaning, we will have unlocked the secret teachings of Jesus, at least according to the Secret Book of James.

And what were the secret teachings of Jesus? If we look at the list of parables, we see how the first and the sixth parable bracket the set of parables we have already covered. The first and sixth parables were two parts of a three parable set ending with the parable of The Prodigal Son. So, it seems as though the first six parables are all being grouped together. Or perhaps 'The Seed' and 'The Building' and 'The Lamps of the Virgins' and 'The Wage of the Workmen' are to be seen as a subset of 'The Shepherds' and the 'Coins.' This seems more likely as the secret readings of 'The Seed' and 'The Building' and 'The Lamps of the Virgins' and 'The Wage of the Workmen' all come down to the closest-packing-of-spheres system that we explored in detail in the third volume.

```
 ┌─────────────────────────────────────┐
 │                                     │
```

Shepherds Seed Building Virgins Workmen Coins

Figure 1. First and sixth parables bracket.

The ordering of the seven parables gives an interesting perspective on the nested nature of the secret teachings. The two bookend parables bracketing the set, 'The Shepherds' and the 'Coins' imply the third member of the triad, The Prodigal Son. In my interpretation, The Prodigal Son is sacrificed by his father when the son returns home. Then, within this set, is a group of four parables that can only be properly understood by someone with knowledge of the closest-packing-of-spheres system. This seems to imply that the secret teaching has two parts. There is the outer part which is about a wayward son returning to his father's home where he is accepted with open arms only to be sacrificed by his supposedly loving father. Within this is the teaching concerning the closest packing of spheres, Genesis, and the planetary gods as detailed in the third volume.

The Woman

However, this description is incomplete because there is a seventh parable titled 'The Woman' that falls last on the list. This would seem to place it on the same level as the parable implied by the first and sixth parables, the parable of The Prodigal Son, with its violent conclusion. This is somewhat interesting on the surface level because come to think of it, where is the woman in the whole prodigal son story anyway? There is nothing mentioned about the father ever having a wife or the brothers ever having a mother. It seems that the man's wife and the brothers' mother had died long before the events in the parable took place, though perhaps she was alive but not mentioned because her existence was deemed inconsequential to the story.

If the order of the parables in the list is intentional, then it would seem to indicate that a proper understanding of the hidden meaning of the parable labeled by the title 'The Woman' should provide the third component of the secret teaching. This part of the secret teaching would be on the same level as the reinterpreted parable of The Prodigal Son and not on the deep mathematical and geometric level delineated by the second, third, fourth and fifth parables.

4

Still, I cannot help but be struck by the manner in which the parables are arranged in pairs. First, there is the bracketing pair of 'The Shepherds' and the 'Coins,' and then there is the first inner pair of 'The Seed' and 'The Building.' For this pair, it is necessary to have some basic knowledge of the closest-packing-of-spheres system, but that is sufficient to understand these two parables' meanings. With the next pair of 'The Lamps of the Virgins' and 'The Wage of the Workmen' to gain a proper understanding of their meanings it is necessary to have a much deeper understanding of both the sphere packing system and astrology and how they interact with the components of the Genesis narrative. These two pairs are nested inside the bracketing pair of 'The Shepherds' and the 'Coins,' and it is this pair which is being paired with the final parable, 'The Woman.' We know that the parables indicated by the labels of 'The Shepherds' and the 'Coins' are two parts of a three parable unit culminating in the parable of The Prodigal Son. So it would not be entirely incorrect to say that with we are dealing with a pair of parables made up of 'The Prodigal Son' and 'The Woman.'

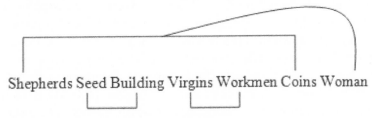

Shepherds Seed Building Virgins Workmen Coins Woman

Figure 2. Pairs among the seven parables.

The first parable we have already solved by turning it inside out but what of 'The Woman'? How much secret meaning can this last simple parable possibly hold?

If you have read the second volume, then you know that this parable has been identified as Matthew 13:33:

33 He spoke another parable to them: The Kingdom of the Heavens is like leaven, which a woman took and hid in three measures of meal until it had been all leavened.
(Mat 13:33 DBY)

There is a near identical version in Luke:

20 And again he said, To what shall I liken the kingdom of God?

21 It is like leaven, which a woman took and hid in three measures of meal until the whole was leavened.
(Luk 13:20-21 DBY)

There is even a version in the Gospel of Thomas:

Jesus said: The Kingdom of the Father is like a certain woman. She took a little leaven, [concealed] it in some dough, and made it into large loaves. Let him who has ears hear.
(GoT 96)

The version from Thomas is especially striking as it includes an admonishment for one with ears to listen, a clear indication that this saying has a significant hidden meaning. But what does the parable mean, even on its surface layer? In the Synoptic versions, the focus is on the leaven, which the woman hides in three measures of flour. So is the parable about the Kingdom of Heaven which expands from something small to something large? If so, then Thomas makes that aspect explicit, a little leaven hidden in dough made large loaves.

There is another difference between the three versions. In the parable found in Matthew, leaven is compared to the Kingdom of Heaven. In Luke, it is compared to the Kingdom of God. In Thomas, the woman is compared to the Kingdom of the Father. The natural assumption is that all three terms are synonymous, and they may well be when used in the Synoptic Gospels, but let us just focus on the manner in which the expressions are used in the Gospel of Thomas.

Thomas uses the term 'Kingdom of the Father' or its equivalent in seven sayings. The term 'Kingdom of Heaven' is found in three sayings. No sayings are using the phrase 'Kingdom of God.'

The Kingdom of Heaven Sayings

The three Kingdom of Heaven sayings are:

Simon Peter said to them: Let Mary leave us, for women are not worthy of the life.

Jesus said: Look, I will guide her that I may make her male, so that she too may become a living spirit resembling you males. For every woman who makes herself male will enter into the Kingdom of Heaven.
(GoT 114)

Jesus said: Blessed are the poor, for yours is the Kingdom of Heaven.
(GoT 54)

The disciples said to Jesus: Tell us what the Kingdom of Heaven is like.
He said to them: It is like a grain of mustard-seed, the smallest of all seeds; but when it falls on the tilled ground, it puts forth a great branch and becomes a shelter for the birds of heaven.
(GoT 20)

The Kingdom of the Father Sayings

The seven Kingdom of the Father sayings are:

His disciples said to him: On what day will the kingdom come?
It will not come while people watch for it; they will not say: Look, here it is, or: Look, there it is, but the Kingdom of the Father is spread out over the earth, and men do not see it.
(GoT 113)

The disciples said to him, Your brothers and your mother are standing outside.
He said to them, Those here who do the will of my Father are my brothers and my mother. It is they who will enter the Kingdom of my Father.
(GoT 99)

Jesus said: The Kingdom of the Father is like a man who wanted to kill a powerful man. He drew a sword in his house and drove it into the wall that he might know his hand would be strong. Then he slew the powerful man.
(GoT 98)

Jesus said: The Kingdom of the [Father] is like a certain woman who was carrying a jar full of meal. While she was walking [on] a road, still some distance from home, the handle of the jar broke, and the meal emptied out behind her on the road. She did not realize it; she had noticed no accident. When she reached her house, she set the jar down and found it empty.
(GoT 97)

Jesus said: The Kingdom of the Father is like a certain woman. She took a little leaven, [hid] it in some dough, and made it into large loaves. Let him who has ears hear.
(GoT 96)

Jesus said: The Kingdom of the Father is like a merchant who had a consignment of merchandise and who discovered a pearl. That merchant was shrewd. He sold the merchandise and bought the pearl alone for himself. You too, seek his unfailing and enduring treasure where no moth comes near to devour, and no worm destroys.
(GoT 76)

Jesus said: The Kingdom of the Father is like a man who had [good] seed. His enemy came by night and sowed weeds among the good seed. The man did not allow them to pull up the weeds; he said to them, 'I am afraid that you will go intending to pull up the weeds and pull up the wheat along with them.' For on the day of the harvest, the weeds will be plainly visible, and they will be pulled up and burned.
(GoT 57)

The Kingdom of the Father

We will return to the Kingdom of Heaven sayings later in this chapter, but for now, given that the saying that corresponds to the parable labeled 'The Woman' is among the Kingdom of the Father sayings, we will focus on these sayings to see what we can learn.

Beginning with the last one on my list, but the first one in the sequence found in Thomas we come to number 57. This saying described the situation when a man had a field in which another man planted some bad seed mixed among the good seed that the owner had planted. The workers wanted to pull up all the plants, but he told them to wait until harvest when the bad plants would be obvious, and they would be burnt. Making this a Kingdom of Father saying adds a layer of sexual innuendo to the whole scenario. The father can never be sure that someone else isn't sowing their seed in his field. He will wait until the bastards are old enough to be recognized before taking action. So the Kingdom of the Father is a realm of paranoia and jealousy.

The next saying, number 76, describes the Kingdom of the Father as being like a man that sold what he had to buy a pearl so that he alone could possess it. The Kingdom of the Father is a place of selfishness and obsessiveness.

Next, we come to the saying that brought us here, number 96. Notice that it a member of a pair of two consecutive Kingdom of the Father sayings with saying number 97 being the second member of the pair. Using a technique I described in the second volume, these two saying can be brought together and merged in the mind's eye. I usually examine the sayings in the reverse order. This gives us:

Jesus said: The Kingdom of the [Father] is like a certain woman who was carrying a jar full of meal. While she was walking [on] a road, still some distance from home, the handle of the jar broke, and the meal emptied out behind her on the road. She did not realize it; she had noticed no accident. When she reached her house, she set the jar down and found it empty.
(GoT 97)

Jesus said: The Kingdom of the Father is like a certain woman. She took a little leaven, [concealed] it in some dough, and made it into large loaves. Let him who has ears hear.
(GoT 96)

First, we must note the obvious similarities. One is about a woman who lost a jar full of meal, the second concerns a woman who hid leaven in a large amount of dough and made from it large loaves of bread. So both are about a woman, and both have something to do with bread. Trying to merge them into a single whole is still difficult.

The actions are described in a somewhat suspicious manner. The woman carrying the jar of meal was almost certainly carrying the jar by its handle, yet she did not notice that it had broken? She also did not notice the jar becoming progressively lighter? And then there is the other woman who is described as hiding the leaven within the dough. That is a somewhat suspicious way to word it. These are the Kingdom of the Father sayings after all. Perhaps a woman came home with an empty jar that was supposed to be filled with flour. The woman told her story, but her husband did not believe her, because he knew what women have been up to when flour turns up missing.

18 The children gather wood, and the fathers kindle the fire, and the women knead their dough, to make cakes to the queen of heaven, and to pour out drink offerings unto other gods, that they may provoke me to anger.
(Jer 7:18 KJV)

He perhaps suspected the woman of baking cakes for the queen of heaven. That is interesting, especially as we have those Kingdom of Heaven sayings. For now, let us see if it is now somehow easier to merge these two sayings. We have the one woman carrying the empty jar with a broken handle and the second woman concealing leaven within dough to bake large loaves. If we merge these two women into a single one, then we have a woman baking large loaves but coming home with an empty jar and a sad story. The two sayings can be merged, but by doing so, the woman's story about the jar must be a lie.

The Kingdom of the Father sayings are shaping up to be of a certain quality, one which is opposed to the queen of heaven and therefore likely to also be in opposition to whatever the Kingdom of Heaven sayings represent. However, as we still have three more Kingdom of the Father sayings, it is possible that the actual nature of the Kingdom of the Father sayings is less negative than it presently appears.

The next two sayings follow directly after the previous two, and they are also in consecutive order. Here they are in reverse order:

The disciples said to Him, Your brothers and your mother are standing outside.

He said to them, Those here who do the will of my Father are my brothers and my mother. It is they who will enter the Kingdom of my Father.
(GoT 99)

Jesus said: The Kingdom of the Father is like a man who wanted to kill a powerful man. He drew a sword in his house and drove it into the wall that he might know his hand would be strong. Then he slew the powerful man.
(GoT 98)

Just looking at number 98, we get the impression that family does not matter. What matters is subordination to the will of the Father. In the other saying, number 99, there is a man, who wishes to kill another man. He tests his own strength by driving his sword through a wall of his house. Then he kills the man.

These also seem impossible to merge. One is about disowning your family, and the other is about killing a man after first thrusting a sword through a wall of your house. The only way I see to merge these two sayings is to assume that the man you want to kill was actually a member of your family whom you had disowned. The thrusting of the sword through the wall of your house means to strike at one within your house which means within your family, who you then kill.

The last Kingdom of the Father saying from the Gospel of Thomas is number 113:

His disciples said to him: On what day will the kingdom come?
It will not come while people watch for it; they will not say: Look, here it is, or: Look, there it is, but the Kingdom of the Father is spread out over the earth, and men do not see it.
(GoT 113)

There is no consecutive Kingdom of the Father saying to merge it with. However, there is the following Kingdom of Heaven saying with which it might possibly be merged.

Simon Peter said to them: Let Mary leave us, for women are not worthy of the life.

Jesus said: Look, I will guide her that I may make her male, so that she too may become a living spirit resembling you males. For every woman who makes herself male will enter into the Kingdom of Heaven.
(GoT 114)

If we are to merge these then we should take the last first, so beginning with number 114, we learn that women don't deserve life. That seems a little strong. Jesus is going to guide Mary so that she can be like the males. Then he says that all women who make themselves male will enter the Kingdom of Heaven.

In the next saying, in reverse order, we learn that the Kingdom of the Father is spread over the earth yet men do not see it. Given what we have learned from saying number 113 where it is stated that women do not deserve life, together with the paranoid possessive aggression found in most of the Kingdom of the Father sayings, it would be more correct to say that while the Kingdom of the Father is spread over the earth and men do not see it, women do. Women suffer because of it.

The Kingdom of Heaven

So, if that is the case, then we have likely determined the nature of the Kingdom of the Father sayings. What about the Kingdom of Heaven sayings? What is their significance? Let us first see what else saying number 114 can tell us.

The most striking feature of this saying is Jesus claiming that he will guide Mary so that she might make herself male. Every commentary I have found concerning this saying makes the assumption that this change in sex has a spiritual or metaphorical interpretation because surely Jesus is not talking about an actual physical changing of genders.

Only, what if he were? Let us suppose that the saying is to be understood that Jesus is going to guide Mary and make her male, in the physical sense of the word. Are there any accounts of women becoming male around the proper era? Well, there is the Fable of Iphis and Ianthe.

It is a rather long fable, the gist of which is: as a wife is about to give birth, her husband demands a boy, threatening to kill the child if it is a girl. The wife gives birth to a girl which she disguises as a boy. The child is named Iphis. She is dressed and raised as a boy.

When Iphis turns thirteen, she becomes engaged to Ianthe, the most beautiful girl in Phaestus. Ianthe and Iphis are in love, but Iphis knows that she cannot fulfill that love. A woman is not to love another woman, so she appeals to her mother for help. The wedding is put off for as long as possible, but they soon run out of excuses. On the night before the wedding, the distraught mother prays to Isis that the goddess finds some way to end her daughter's misery. When she arises from the altar, Iphis has been transformed into a man.

Isis, the Great Mother, performs a gender change from female to male. The fable is found in Ovid's Metamorphoses: (Dryden, 1751)

> *But having done whate'er she could devise,*
> *And empty'd all her magazine of lies,*
> *The time approach'd; the next ensuing day*
> *The fatal secret must to light betray.*
> *Then Telethusa had recourse to pray'r,*
> *She, and her daughter with dishevel'd hair;*
> *Trembling with fear, great Isis they ador'd,*
> *Embrac'd her altar, and her aid implor'd.*

> *Fair queen, who dost on fruitful Egypt smile,*
> *Who sway'st the sceptre of the Pharian isle,*
> *And sev'n-fold falls of disemboguing Nile,*
> *Relieve, in this our last distress, she said,*
> *A suppliant mother, and a mournful maid.*
> *Thou, Goddess, thou wert present to my sight;*
> *Reveal'd I saw thee by thy own fair light:*
> *I saw thee in my dream, as now I see,*
> *With all thy marks of awful majesty:*
> *The glorious train that compass'd thee around;*
> *And heard the hollow timbrels holy sound.*
> *Thy words I noted, which I still retain;*
> *Let not thy sacred oracles be vain.*
> *That Iphis lives, that I myself am free*
> *From shame, and punishment, I owe to thee.*
> *On thy protection all our hopes depend.*
> *Thy counsel sav'd us, let thy pow'r defend.*

Her tears pursu'd her words; and while she spoke,
The Goddess nodded, and her altar shook:
The temple doors, as with a blast of wind,
Were heard to clap; the lunar horns that bind
The brows of Isis cast a blaze around;
The trembling timbrel made a murm'ring sound.

Some hopes these happy omens did impart;
Forth went the mother with a beating heart:
Not much in fear, nor fully satisfy'd;
But Iphis follow'd with a larger stride:
The whiteness of her skin forsook her face;
Her looks embolden'd with an awful grace;
Her features, and her strength together grew,
And her long hair to curling locks withdrew.
Her sparkling eyes with manly vigour shone,
Big was her voice, audacious was her tone.
The latent parts, at length reveal'd, began
To shoot, and spread, and burnish into man.
The maid becomes a youth; no more delay
Your vows, but look, and confidently pay.
Their gifts the parents to the temple bear:
The votive tables this inscription wear;
Iphis the man, has to the Goddess paid
The vows, that Iphis offer'd when a maid.

Now when the star of day had shewn his face,
Venus and Juno with their presence grace
The nuptial rites, and Hymen from above
Descending to complete their happy love;
The Gods of marriage lend their mutual aid;
And the warm youth enjoys the lovely maid.
(From The Fable of IPHIS and IANTHE.
By Mr. DRYDEN.)

Here we have a legendary account of a woman being turned miraculously into a man by the goddess Isis. So changing gender was not a foreign concept during that distant age and if you wanted it done, you went to the Queen of Heaven.

Returning to the saying:

Simon Peter said to them, Mary should leave us, for females are not worthy of life.

Why is Peter so upset? Because Jesus is revealing the inner secrets of his teachings and Mary is there, listening with the other disciples. Mary should not have access to this knowledge because she is a woman. With that in mind let us examine a piece of text from the Library of Photius, an account from Diodorus Siculus (Oldfather, 1933):

There was an Epidaurian child, named Callo, orphaned of both her parents, who was supposed to be a girl. Now the orifice with which women are naturally provided had in her case no opening, but beside the so-called pecten [pubis] she had from birth a perforation through which she excreted the liquid residues.

On reaching maturity she became the wife of a fellow-citizen. For two years she lived with him, and since she was incapable of intercourse as a woman, she was obliged to submit to unnatural embraces. Later a tumour appeared on her genitals and because it gave rise to great pain a number of physicians were called in. None of the others would take the responsibility for treating her, but a certain apothecary, who offered to cure her, cut into the swollen area, whereupon a man's privates were protruded, namely testicles and an imperforate penis. While all the others stood amazed at the extraordinary event, the apothecary took steps to remedy the remaining deficiencies. First of all, cutting into the glans, he made a passage into the urethra, and inserting a silver catheter drew off the liquid residues. Then, by scarifying the perforated area, he brought the parts together. After achieving a cure in this manner he demanded double fees, saying that he had received a female invalid and made her into a healthy young man.

Callo laid aside her loom-shuttles and all other instruments of woman's work, and taking in their stead the garb and status of a man, changed her name (by adding a single letter, N, at the end) to Callon. It is stated by some that before changing to man's form she had been a priestess of Demeter, and that because she had witnessed things not to be seen by a man, she was brought for trial for impiety.

(Diodorus Siculus, XXXII 11 Photius, Library, codex 244, 378b])

Callo as a woman had been a priestess in the cult of Demeter. When she became a man, she was brought to trial, because the secrets she, or rather he, now knew were not lawful for a man to know. Compare this with Peter's attitude toward Mary.

Another interesting fact to keep in mind is that the goddess Demeter is the Greek equivalent of Isis, which means she is also a Queen of Heaven.

One of the critical sayings of the Gospel of Thomas is:

Jesus said: Recognize what is before you, and what is hidden from you will be revealed to you; for there is nothing hidden that will not be made manifest.
(GoT 5)

I find this saying especially helpful for decrypting saying number 114. Simon Peter is upset that May might learn some of the secrets that are reserved for men. Jesus claims that he will assist Mary so that she can be like the males. What about the opposite situation? We have seen how a woman who became male was charged with impiety. Where there ever examples of men who wanted to learn the secrets of a goddess cult but who first had to give up their male gender?

There was a goddess cult that spread to Greece in the sixth century BC. This cult worshiped the goddess Cybele, who would come to be known in Rome as the Magna Mater, the Great Mother. In addition to priestesses and temple prostitutes, this goddess cult had castrated priests known as the Galli. Lucian wrote of them in his work *On the Syrian Goddess* (Strong, 1913):

During these days they are made Galli. As the Galli sing and celebrate their orgies, frenzy falls on many of them and many who had come as mere spectators afterwards are found to have committed the great act. I will narrate what they do. Any young man who has resolved on this action, strips off his clothes, and with a loud shout bursts into the midst of the crowd, and picks up a sword from a number of swords which I suppose have been kept ready for many years for this purpose. He takes it and castrates himself and then runs wild through the city, bearing in his hands what he has cut off. He casts it into any house at will, and from this house he

receives women's raiment and ornaments. Thus they act during their ceremonies of castration.
Chapter 51

In his *On the Nature of Things*, the poet Lucretius gives another description of the Galli (Bailey, 1921):

To her [the Idean Mother] do they assign the Galli, the emasculate, since thus they wish to show that men who violate the majesty of the mother and have proved ingrate to parents are to be judged unfit to give unto the shores of light a living progeny. The Galli come: and hollow cymbals, tight-skinned tambourines resound around to bangings of their hands; The fierce horns threaten with a raucous bray; The tubed pipe excites their maddened minds in Phrygian measures; they bear before them knives, wild emblems of their frenzy, which have power the rabble's ingrate heads and impious hearts to panic with terror of the goddess' might.

There is also Carmina 53 by Catullus (Burton, 1928):

Over the vast main borne by swift-sailing ship, Attis, as with hasty hurried foot he reached the Phrygian wood and gained the tree-girt gloomy sanctuary of the Goddess, there roused by rabid rage and mind astray, with sharp-edged flint downwards dashed his burden of virility. Then as he felt his limbs were left without their manhood, and the fresh-spilt blood staining the soil, with bloodless hand she hastily took a tambour light to hold, your taborine, Cybele, your initiate rite, and with feeble fingers beating the hollowed bullock's back, she rose up quivering thus to chant to her companions.

The most entertaining description is contained within *The Golden Ass* by Apuleius. A little context is necessary to make sense of the scene below. The novel's protagonist, Lucius, has accidentally turned himself into an ass. He has various adventures including being sold in an auction to a eunuch priest of the goddess (Kline, 2013):

'This is no ass you see before you, it's a bell-wether of the flock, never a biter or kicker, but gentle as a lamb for any task. You'd

think,' said the auctioneer, 'that inside this ass's hide lived the mildest of human beings. It's not hard to prove either: just stick your face between his back legs, and you'll easily demonstrate his truly passive nature.'

The auctioneer was having fun at the eunuch's expense, but the latter got the point of the joke and swore with feigned indignation: 'You lunatic, you deaf and dumb corpse of an auctioneer! I call on the all-powerful, the all-creating goddess, Syrian Atagartis; and holy Sabazius too, and Ma of Commagene; on Idaean Mother Cybele and her consort Attis; on Lady Astarte and her consort Adonis; may they strike you blind as well for tormenting me with your scurrilous jests. Do you think I'd entrust the goddess, you fool, to some savage creature that might tumble her sacred image from its back, and be forced to run round like a servant-girl, hair streaming in the wind, to find a doctor for my goddess as she lay there on the ground?'

Hearing that, it crossed my mind to start leaping around like mad, so he'd give up the whole idea of buying me when he saw how savage I was when roused. But that eager purchaser thwarted my scheme, by paying a price on the nail that my owner, of course, being doubtless thoroughly sick and tired of me, swiftly and joyfully accepted: less than a single gold piece, seventeen denarii. He handed me over at once with the halter, made of common broom, to this Philebus for such was the name of the man who was my new owner.

Taking possession of his new follower, he dragged me home with him, and reaching the doorway cried: 'Look what a pretty slave I've bought you, girls!' The 'girls' were his troop of eunuchs who began dancing in delight, raising a dissonant clamour with tuneless, shrill, effeminate cries, thinking no doubt his purchase was a slave-boy ready to do them service. But on seeing me, no doe replacing a sacrificial virgin, but an ass instead of a boy, they turned up their noses, and made caustic remarks to their leader.

'Here's no slave,' one cried, 'but a husband of your own.' And 'Oh,' called another, 'don't swallow that little morsel all by yourself, give your little doves the occasional bite.' Then amidst the banter they tied me to the manger.

Now in that house was a corpulent lad, a fine flute-player, bought in the slave-market with the funds from their begging-plate, who circled around playing his pipes when they lead the goddess

*about, but at home played the part of concubine, sharing himself
around.*
    The Golden Ass Book VIII

At the end of the book, Lucius prays to the goddess Isis that he
might be returned to his human form. The goddess answers and
reveals her true nature:

*'Behold, Lucius, here I am, moved by your prayer, I, mother of
all Nature and mistress of the elements, first-born of the ages and
greatest of powers divine, queen of the dead, and queen of the
immortals, all gods and goddesses in a single form; who with a
gesture commands heaven's glittering summit, the wholesome ocean
breezes, the underworld's mournful silence; whose sole divinity is
worshipped in differing forms, with varying rites, under many names,
by all the world. There, at Pessinus, the Phrygians, first-born of men,
call me Cybele, Mother of the Gods; in Attica, a people sprung from
their own soil name me Cecropian Minerva; in sea-girt Cyprus I am
Paphian Venus; Dictynna-Diana to the Cretan archers; Stygian
Proserpine to the three-tongued Sicilians; at Eleusis, ancient Ceres;
Juno to some, to others Bellona, Hecate, Rhamnusia; while the races
of both Ethiopias, first to be lit at dawn by the risen Sun's divine
rays, and the Egyptians too, deep in arcane lore, worship me with
my own rites, and call me by my true name, royal Isis.'*
    The Golden Ass Book XI

So to Apuleius, at least, Cybele was just another form of Isis,
the Queen of Heaven. As a member of the cult of Cybele, a man
could become a high priest but only if he castrated himself. Cybele
became an official state goddess in 204 BC, but the only Galli in
Rome were foreigners or slaves as Roman citizens who could not
legally be castrated. Emperor Claudius lifted this restriction. In time,
Emperor Domitian reaffirmed that Roman citizens cannot undergo
castration and alternative means of sacrifice were devised. For our
interests, it is enough to know that it was a popular goddess religion
which allowed men to become priests if they castrated themselves.
This is, I claim, what is hidden from us in the description of Simon
Peter attempting to banish Mary until Jesus promises to help her
become male.
    Let us look at the other Kingdom of Heaven sayings:

The disciples said to Jesus: Tell us what the Kingdom of Heaven is like.

He said to them: It is like a grain of mustard-seed, the smallest of all seeds; but when it falls on the tilled ground, it puts forth a great branch and becomes shelter for the birds of heaven.
(GoT 20)

Saying 20 also can be read as being fairly phallic centered, with its description of the 'great branch' that is the result of the mustard seed falling on the tilled ground. What to say about saying 54?

The Profitability of Complete Circumcision

Jesus said: Blessed are the poor, for yours is the Kingdom of Heaven.
(GoT 54)

Here we have nothing phallic or connected to castration. However, there is the fallback technique of merging consecutive sayings. The previous saying is below:

His disciples said to Him, Is circumcision beneficial or not?
He said to them, If it were beneficial, their father would beget them already circumcised from their mother. Rather, the true circumcision in spirit has become completely profitable.
(GoT 53)

In saying 54, we learn that the poor are blessed. In 53, we discover that the true circumcision in spirit is completely profitable. One saying concerns the poor while the second discusses profitability. Notice also how the true circumcision is 'completely' profitable. That is a strange way to describe profitability. Generally, something is more profitable or very profitable. It seems to me that the saying is hinting that the term 'completely' has more to do with circumcision than with profitability. In other words, the true circumcision is complete circumcision. This brings all three Kingdom of Heaven sayings together in that they all contain either phallic symbolism or castration symbolism, though in the case of 54 it only becomes apparent when this saying is merged with a consecutive saying.

Kingdom versus Kingdom

This gives us two sets of sayings associated with two separate kingdoms. One is the Kingdom of the Father, and the other is the Kingdom of Heaven. The Kingdom of Heaven sayings are associated with Cybele who is apparently just another form of Isis, the Queen of Heaven. The Kingdom of the Father is referenced by seven sayings that apparently present the viewpoint of a jealous and paranoid man that does not trust women. It seems as though these two groups of sayings represent two opposing groups: the father versus the goddess. As for why the father might be opposed to the goddess we need only to look at her form of worship which involves men castrating themselves. Fathers are concerned with bloodlines and building families. They are naturally concerned with cults which lure young men and seduce them into castrating themselves because these young men are the sons of fathers.

New Wine into Old Skins

What connections do we see linking the Jesus found within the Synoptic Gospels to the goddess cult? There is a peculiar saying found in all three Synoptic Gospels as well as in Thomas. The saying concerns wineskins and the inadvisability of putting new wine into old wineskins.

22 And no one puts new wine into old skins; otherwise the wine bursts the skins, and the wine is poured out, and the skins will be destroyed; but new wine is to be put into new skins.
(Mar 2:22 DBY)

17 Nor do men put new wine into old skins, otherwise the skins burst and the wine is poured out, and the skins will be destroyed; but they put new wine into new skins, and both are preserved together.
(Mat 9:17 DBY)

37 And no one puts new wine into old skins, otherwise the new wine will burst the skins, and it will be poured out, and the skins will be destroyed;

21

38 but new wine is to be put into new skins, and both are preserved.

39 And no one having drunk old wine straightway wishes for new, for he says, The old is better.

(Luk 5:37-39 DBY)

Jesus said: A person cannot mount two horses or draw two bows. And a slave cannot serve two masters, but truly will honor the one and scoff at the other. No person drinks old wine and immediately desires to drink new wine. And new wine is not put into old wineskins lest they burst. And old wine is not put into new wineskins lest it goes bad. And old patches are not sewed to new garments, for a rip will develop.

(GoT 47)

Notice how Matthew follows Mark closely while Luke mixes things up by adding the bit about people preferring old wine to new. Then there is Thomas which mixes in several sets of pairs. Thomas takes Luke's addition and then reveals a new bit of information, why old wine is not put in new wineskins. Still, in these instances, it is difficult to discern any secret meaning. We might have better luck if we explored the various contexts of the different versions.

14 As he walked along, he saw Levi son of Alphaeus sitting at the tax collector's booth. "Follow me," Jesus told him, and Levi got up and followed him.

15 While Jesus was having dinner at Levi's house, many tax collectors and "sinners" were eating with him and his disciples, for there were many who followed him.

16 When the teachers of the law who were Pharisees saw him eating with the "sinners" and tax collectors, they asked his disciples: "Why does he eat with tax collectors and 'sinners'?"

17 On hearing this, Jesus said to them, "It is not the healthy who need a doctor, but the sick. I have not come to call the righteous, but sinners."

18 Now John's disciples and the Pharisees were fasting. Some people came and asked Jesus, "How is it that John's disciples and the disciples of the Pharisees are fasting, but yours are not?"

19 Jesus answered, "How can the guests of the bridegroom fast while he is with them? They cannot, so long as they have him with them.

20 But the time will come when the bridegroom will be taken from them, and on that day they will fast.

21 "No one sews a patch of unshrunk cloth on an old garment. If he does, the new piece will pull away from the old, making the tear worse.

22 And no one pours new wine into old wineskins. If he does, the wine will burst the skins, and both the wine and the wineskins will be ruined. No, he pours new wine into new wineskins."

23 One Sabbath Jesus was going through the grainfields, and as his disciples walked along, they began to pick some heads of grain.

(Mar 2:14-23 NIV)

Looking first at Mark, given that it was the first written, we see the scene beginning with Jesus telling Levi the tax collector to follow him. Jesus then has dinner at Levi's house, together with many tax collectors and sinners. The Pharisees ask why John's and the Pharisees' disciples fast, but Jesus and his followers do not. Jesus gives the example of not patching an old garment with a new unshrunk patch. Jesus and his way is apparently the new piece of cloth, while Judaism is the old garment. Then Jesus gives the example of old wine being put into new wineskins. The new wine is I assume the new teaching of Jesus, while the new wineskins are the outer forms of piety that he and his followers observe. Then after the conclusion of this section, Jesus and his gang are off to the grainfields.

Next, we will look at the same section from Luke:

27 After this, Jesus went out and saw a tax collector by the name of Levi sitting at his tax booth. "Follow me," Jesus said to him,

28 and Levi got up, left everything and followed him.

29 Then Levi held a great banquet for Jesus at his house, and a large crowd of tax collectors and others were eating with them.

30 But the Pharisees and the teachers of the law who belonged to their sect complained to his disciples, "Why do you eat and drink with tax collectors and 'sinners'?"

31 Jesus answered them, "It is not the healthy who need a doctor, but the sick.

32 I have not come to call the righteous, but sinners to repentance."

33 They said to him, "John's disciples often fast and pray, and so do the disciples of the Pharisees, but yours go on eating and drinking."

34 Jesus answered, "Can you make the guests of the bridegroom fast while he is with them?

35 But the time will come when the bridegroom will be taken from them; in those days they will fast."

36 He told them this parable: "No one tears a patch from a new garment and sews it on an old one. If he does, he will have torn the new garment, and the patch from the new will not match the old.

37 And no one pours new wine into old wineskins. If he does, the new wine will burst the skins, the wine will run out and the wineskins will be ruined.

38 No, new wine must be poured into new wineskins.

39 And no one after drinking old wine wants the new, for he says, 'The old is better.'"

Luke 6:1 One Sabbath Jesus was going through the grainfields, and his disciples began to pick some heads of grain, rub them in their hands and eat the kernels.

(Luk 5:27-1 NIV)

Luke follows Mark quite closely. One difference is that in Luke's version of the new patch on an old garment, the text mentions that taking the new patch from a new garment will damage the new and will not match the old. It is also in Luke that mention is made of the fact no one wants to drink new wine after drinking old because the old wine will be judged to be better. This could be taken to mean that those who knew the old Jewish teachers were not especially interested in what Jesus had to teach. Finally at the end of the section, Luke also has Jesus and the disciples going through a grainfield.

Now let us look at the section from Matthew:

9 As Jesus went on from there, he saw a man named Matthew sitting at the tax collector's booth. "Follow me," he told him, and Matthew got up and followed him.

10 While Jesus was having dinner at Matthew's house, many tax collectors and "sinners" came and ate with him and his disciples.

11 When the Pharisees saw this, they asked his disciples, "Why does your teacher eat with tax collectors and 'sinners'?"

12 On hearing this, Jesus said, "It is not the healthy who need a doctor, but the sick.

13 But go and learn what this means: 'I desire mercy, not sacrifice.' For I have not come to call the righteous, but sinners."

14 Then John's disciples came and asked him, "How is it that we and the Pharisees fast, but your disciples do not fast?"

15 Jesus answered, "How can the guests of the bridegroom mourn while he is with them? The time will come when the bridegroom will be taken from them; then they will fast.

16 "No one sews a patch of unshrunk cloth on an old garment, for the patch will pull away from the garment, making the tear worse.

17 Neither do men pour new wine into old wineskins. If they do, the skins will burst, the wine will run out and the wineskins will be ruined. No, they pour new wine into new wineskins, and both are preserved."

18 While he was saying this, a ruler came and knelt before him and said, "My daughter has just died. But come and put your hand on her, and she will live."

(Mat 9:9-18 NIV)

In Matthew, the most significant change from Mark is the identification of the tax collector not as Levi son of Alphaeus, but simply as Matthew. The next difference is what happens immediately after this section. Usually, this is followed by Jesus and his followers walking through a grainfield. In Matthew, it is followed by the miracle of Jairus' daughter. The man who comes before Jesus in Matthew is identified simply as a ruler. We should first examine Mark to see the miracle's earliest version.

Saving the Daughter of Jairus

22 Then one of the synagogue rulers, named Jairus, came there. Seeing Jesus, he fell at his feet

23 and pleaded earnestly with him, "My little daughter is dying. Please come and put your hands on her so that she will be healed and live."

24 So Jesus went with him. A large crowd followed and pressed around him.

25 And a woman was there who had been subject to bleeding for twelve years.

26 She had suffered a great deal under the care of many doctors and had spent all she had, yet instead of getting better she grew worse.

27 When she heard about Jesus, she came up behind him in the crowd and touched his cloak,

28 because she thought, "If I just touch his clothes, I will be healed."

29 Immediately her bleeding stopped and she felt in her body that she was freed from her suffering.

30 At once Jesus realized that power had gone out from him. He turned around in the crowd and asked, "Who touched my clothes?"

31 "You see the people crowding against you," his disciples answered, "and yet you can ask, 'Who touched me?'"

32 But Jesus kept looking around to see who had done it.

33 Then the woman, knowing what had happened to her, came and fell at his feet and, trembling with fear, told him the whole truth.

34 He said to her, "Daughter, your faith has healed you. Go in peace and be freed from your suffering."

35 While Jesus was still speaking, some men came from the house of Jairus, the synagogue ruler. "Your daughter is dead," they said. "Why bother the teacher any more?"

36 Ignoring what they said, Jesus told the synagogue ruler, "Don't be afraid; just believe."

37 He did not let anyone follow him except Peter, James and John the brother of James.

38 When they came to the home of the synagogue ruler, Jesus saw a commotion, with people crying and wailing loudly.

39 He went in and said to them, "Why all this commotion and wailing? The child is not dead but asleep."

40 But they laughed at him. After he put them all out, he took the child's father and mother and the disciples who were with him, and went in where the child was.

41 He took her by the hand and said to her, "Talitha koum!" (which means, "Little girl, I say to you, get up!").

42 Immediately the girl stood up and walked around (she was twelve years old). At this they were completely astonished.

43 He gave strict orders not to let anyone know about this, and told them to give her something to eat.

(Mar 5:22-43 NIV)

In this version we see how it got its name as the father of the dying girl is identified as Jairus. We also recognize that this is a two-part miracle as Jesus also heals the hemorrhaging woman. Finally, Jesus arrives at Jairus' home where the people are crying and wailing. Jesus says that the girl is sleeping and not dead, after which he heals her.

Luke follows Mark rather closely:

41 Then a man named Jairus, a ruler of the synagogue, came and fell at Jesus' feet, pleading with him to come to his house

42 because his only daughter, a girl of about twelve, was dying. As Jesus was on his way, the crowds almost crushed him.

43 And a woman was there who had been subject to bleeding for twelve years, but no one could heal her.

44 She came up behind him and touched the edge of his cloak, and immediately her bleeding stopped.

45 "Who touched me?" Jesus asked. When they all denied it, Peter said, "Master, the people are crowding and pressing against you."

46 But Jesus said, "Someone touched me; I know that power has gone out from me."

47 Then the woman, seeing that she could not go unnoticed, came trembling and fell at his feet. In the presence of all the people, she told why she had touched him and how she had been instantly healed.

48 Then he said to her, "Daughter, your faith has healed you. Go in peace."

49 While Jesus was still speaking, someone came from the house of Jairus, the synagogue ruler. "Your daughter is dead," he said. "Don't bother the teacher any more."

50 Hearing this, Jesus said to Jairus, "Don't be afraid; just believe, and she will be healed."

51 When he arrived at the house of Jairus, he did not let anyone go in with him except Peter, John and James, and the child's father and mother.

52 Meanwhile, all the people were wailing and mourning for her. "Stop wailing," Jesus said. "She is not dead but asleep."

53 They laughed at him, knowing that she was dead.

54 But he took her by the hand and said, "My child, get up!"

55 Her spirit returned, and at once she stood up. Then Jesus told them to give her something to eat.

56 Her parents were astonished, but he ordered them not to tell anyone what had happened.

(Luk 8:41-56 NIV)

Again, Luke followed Mark quite closely. They are nearly identical though Luke has fewer details than Mark.

Finally, we come to Matthew's version:

18 While he was saying this, a ruler came and knelt before him and said, "My daughter has just died. But come and put your hand on her, and she will live."

19 Jesus got up and went with him, and so did his disciples.

20 Just then a woman who had been subject to bleeding for twelve years came up behind him and touched the edge of his cloak.

21 She said to herself, "If I only touch his cloak, I will be healed."

22 Jesus turned and saw her. "Take heart, daughter," he said, "your faith has healed you." And the woman was healed from that moment.

23 When Jesus entered the ruler's house and saw the flute players and the noisy crowd,

24 he said, "Go away. The girl is not dead but asleep." But they laughed at him.

25 After the crowd had been put outside, he went in and took the girl by the hand, and she got up.

(Mat 9:18-25 NIV)

This version is shorter than the version found in Mark. There is a rule that the shorter version is generally assumed to be earlier. However, Mark is seen as the earlier Gospel, yet Matthew's version is much shorter and simpler than both Mark and Luke's. There are some other significant changes as well. In Matthew's version, the ruler informs Jesus that his daughter has already died. Also, the description of Jesus and the hemorrhaging woman is different in that there is no mention of a crowd pushing and pressing against Jesus and his followers. In addition, Jesus is described as entering the house of the ruler alone. The most significant difference, however, is the description of the crowd. In both Mark and Luke, the crowd is described as wailing and mourning the death of the little girl while in Matthew there are flute players and a noisy crowd. There is no mention of mourning. It seems more like a celebration.

Indeed the playing of the flute is often associated with Cybele and her rites and celebrations.

The following is from Mirek Polisensky's *The Language and Origin of the Etruscans* (Polišenský, 1991) 1991, pg.157.

Flute-players in Mesopotamia were eunuchs who played during the procession held on the occasion of the New Year celebration. These eunuchs were Ishtar's priests and they were called assinu, "effeminate", which points to the same character as Etr. 0anasa, "womb", for Etruscan artists dancing and playing flute during processions, who also were called by the name *ister.

So the celebrations of Cybele and those of Ishtar were both associated with flute music. These goddess cults were connected to the female reproductive organs. For the moment let us shift our attention from the daughter of Jairus and instead focus on the hemorrhaging woman. What information does the Bible give us about how her condition would affect her life?

The Bleeding Woman

19 When a woman has her regular flow of blood, the impurity of her monthly period will last seven days, and anyone who touches her will be unclean till evening.

20 Anything she lies on during her period will be unclean, and anything she sits on will be unclean.

21 Whoever touches her bed must wash his clothes and bathe with water, and he will be unclean till evening.

22 Whoever touches anything she sits on must wash his clothes and bathe with water, and he will be unclean till evening.

23 Whether it is the bed or anything she was sitting on, when anyone touches it, he will be unclean till evening.

24 If a man lies with her and her monthly flow touches him, he will be unclean for seven days; any bed he lies on will be unclean.

25 When a woman has a discharge of blood for many days at a time other than her monthly period or has a discharge that continues beyond her period, she will be unclean as long as she has the discharge, just as in the days of her period.

26 Any bed she lies on while her discharge continues will be unclean, as is her bed during her monthly period, and anything she sits on will be unclean, as during her period.

27 Whoever touches them will be unclean; he must wash his clothes and bathe with water, and he will be unclean till evening.

(Lev 15:19-27 NIV)

Apparently, this woman spent her entire life ritually unclean. Well, not her entire life, because Luke and Mark both mention that she had been bleeding for twelve years. This number is significant because the little girl is identified as being twelve years old. What we need to do is to merge the little girl and the hemorrhaging woman together. They are the same. The little girl is dead. She is a woman now, she bleeds and becomes unclean. Jesus heals her? How?

The secret is concealed within the interactions between Jesus and the bleeding woman:

42 ... As Jesus was on his way, the crowds almost crushed him.

43 And a woman was there who had been subject to bleeding for twelve years, but no one could heal her.

44 She came up behind him and touched the edge of his cloak, and immediately her bleeding stopped.

45 "Who touched me?" Jesus asked. When they all denied it, Peter said, "Master, the people are crowding and pressing against you."

46 But Jesus said, "Someone touched me; I know that power has gone out from me."

47 Then the woman, seeing that she could not go unnoticed, came trembling and fell at his feet. In the presence of all the people, she told why she had touched him and how she had been instantly healed.

48 Then he said to her, "Daughter, your faith has healed you. Go in peace."
(Luk 8:42-48 NIV)

24 ... A large crowd followed and pressed around him.
25 And a woman was there who had been subject to bleeding for twelve years.
26 She had suffered a great deal under the care of many doctors and had spent all she had, yet instead of getting better she grew worse.
27 When she heard about Jesus, she came up behind him in the crowd and touched his cloak,
28 because she thought, "If I just touch his clothes, I will be healed."
29 Immediately her bleeding stopped and she felt in her body that she was freed from her suffering.
30 At once Jesus realized that power had gone out from him. He turned around in the crowd and asked, "Who touched my clothes?"
31 "You see the people crowding against you," his disciples answered, "and yet you can ask, 'Who touched me?'"
32 But Jesus kept looking around to see who had done it.
33 Then the woman, knowing what had happened to her, came and fell at his feet and, trembling with fear, told him the whole truth.
34 He said to her, "Daughter, your faith has healed you. Go in peace and be freed from your suffering."
(Mar 5:24-34 NIV)

We must consider the manipulations required by GoT saying 22: *Jesus said to them: When you make the two one, and when you make the inside as the outside, and the outside as the inside...*
Jesus is almost being crushed by the crowd as it pushes on him. The bleeding woman thinks to herself that if she touches his robe, or more specifically its edge, that she would be healed. She manages to do so, but Jesus feels the power flow out of him. He asks who touched him, but his disciples point out that many people are touching him in the crowd. The woman then comes forward and admits that it was she who done it. Jesus tells her that her faith has healed her and she should go in peace.

We need to flip several modalities. We need to flip Jesus to the woman, and the power that he feels going out from him is actually blood flowing out from the woman's body and into the fabric. Then we need to flip above and below because the miracle did not happen when her hand touched the fabric, but when the fabric touches her genitals. And just as Jesus is pressed upon by the crowd, the fabric should be bound tightly against the groin, so that no one can witness the transfer of blood. In this manner, the curse can be concealed. The woman needs only to have faith and to go about her business normally with no one the wiser.

The same holds true for the daughter of Jairus. Jesus allowed the little girl to continue being a little girl without the worries associated with being ritually unclean. He perhaps tore a strip from the edge of his robe and applied it to her body.

41 He took her by the hand and said to her, "Talitha koum!" (which means, "Little girl, I say to you, get up!").

42 Immediately the girl stood up and walked around (she was twelve years old). At this they were completely astonished.

43 He gave strict orders not to let anyone know about this, and told them to give her something to eat.
(Mar 5:41-43 NIV)

Finally, we come full circle to the saying that started this all:

17 Neither do men pour new wine into old wineskins. If they do, the skins will burst, the wine will run out and the wineskins will be ruined. No, they pour new wine into new wineskins, and both are preserved.
(Mat 9:17 NIV)

Seeing as this saying about wineskins directly precedes the miracle of Jairus's daughter in Matthew, the one version that had flutes being played, this saying is likely associated with the whole theme of menstrual blood. Indeed, it could very well serve as a garbled explanation for why menstruation occurs. The blood-flow is the result of old eggs being flushed away from the walls of the uterus. Or old wine is washing away the old wineskins so that the new wine can be housed in new wineskins. There is obviously a switch in modality between inner and outer where a wineskin with wine inside becomes an egg with blood outside.

The Maiden and the Cursed Fig Tree

There is another example of this type of miracle story with a probable connection to goddess worship. We begin with Jesus cursing a fig tree:

12 The next day as they were leaving Bethany, Jesus was hungry.

13 Seeing in the distance a fig tree in leaf, he went to find out if it had any fruit. When he reached it, he found nothing but leaves, because it was not the season for figs.

14 Then he said to the tree, "May no one ever eat fruit from you again." And his disciples heard him say it.

15 On reaching Jerusalem, Jesus entered the temple area and began driving out those who were buying and selling there. He overturned the tables of the money changers and the benches of those selling doves,

16 and would not allow anyone to carry merchandise through the temple courts.

17 And as he taught them, he said, "Is it not written: " 'My house will be called a house of prayer for all nations'? But you have made it 'a den of robbers.' "

18 The chief priests and the teachers of the law heard this and began looking for a way to kill him, for they feared him, because the whole crowd was amazed at his teaching.

19 When evening came, they went out of the city.

20 In the morning, as they went along, they saw the fig tree withered from the roots.

21 Peter remembered and said to Jesus, "Rabbi, look! The fig tree you cursed has withered!"

22 "Have faith in God," Jesus answered.

23 "I tell you the truth, if anyone says to this mountain, 'Go, throw yourself into the sea,' and does not doubt in his heart but believes that what he says will happen, it will be done for him.

(Mar 11:12-23 NIV)

That is a strange story. The usual explanation is that the fig tree represents Israel which was not following God's commandments and would soon be punished. The insertion of the overturning the tables of the money changers at the temple between the curse and the reveal makes such a reading fairly obvious.

18 Early in the morning, as he was on his way back to the city, he was hungry.

19 Seeing a fig tree by the road, he went up to it but found nothing on it except leaves. Then he said to it, "May you never bear fruit again!" Immediately the tree withered.

20 When the disciples saw this, they were amazed. "How did the fig tree wither so quickly?" they asked.

21 Jesus replied, "I tell you the truth, if you have faith and do not doubt, not only can you do what was done to the fig tree, but also you can say to this mountain, 'Go, throw yourself into the sea,' and it will be done.

22 If you believe, you will receive whatever you ask for in prayer."

(Mat 21:18-22 NIV)

Matthew has removed the break and has the curse take place immediately. Both versions close with the promise that if you have total faith, your prayers will come true. Then we have the version from Luke, which is written in the form of a parable rather than a miracle although the subject matter is the same:

4 Or those eighteen who died when the tower in Siloam fell on them--do you think they were more guilty than all the others living in Jerusalem?

5 I tell you, no! But unless you repent, you too will all perish."

6 Then he told this parable: "A man had a fig tree, planted in his vineyard, and he went to look for fruit on it, but did not find any.

7 So he said to the man who took care of the vineyard, 'For three years now I've been coming to look for fruit on this fig tree and haven't found any. Cut it down! Why should it use up the soil?'

8 " 'Sir,' the man replied, 'leave it alone for one more year, and I'll dig around it and fertilize it.

9 If it bears fruit next year, fine! If not, then cut it down.'"

10 On a Sabbath Jesus was teaching in one of the synagogues,

11 and a woman was there who had been crippled by a spirit for eighteen years. She was bent over and could not straighten up at all.

12 When Jesus saw her, he called her forward and said to her, "Woman, you are set free from your infirmity."

13 Then he put his hands on her, and immediately she straightened up and praised God.

14 Indignant because Jesus had healed on the Sabbath, the synagogue ruler said to the people, "There are six days for work. So come and be healed on those days, not on the Sabbath."

15 The Lord answered him, "You hypocrites! Doesn't each of you on the Sabbath untie his ox or donkey from the stall and lead it out to give it water?

16 Then should not this woman, a daughter of Abraham, whom Satan has kept bound for eighteen long years, be set free on the Sabbath day from what bound her?"

17 When he said this, all his opponents were humiliated, but the people were delighted with all the wonderful things he was doing.

18 Then Jesus asked, "What is the kingdom of God like? What shall I compare it to?

19 It is like a mustard seed, which a man took and planted in his garden. It grew and became a tree, and the birds of the air perched in its branches."

20 Again he asked, "What shall I compare the kingdom of God to?

21 It is like yeast that a woman took and mixed into a large amount of flour until it worked all through the dough."

(Luk 13:4-21 NIV)

So, what is the secret hidden in this section?

There are several curious features of the text which stand out. First is the repetition of the number eighteen. Eighteen people died when the tower in Siloam collapsed on them and then the eighteen years that this woman has been unable to walk straight. The length of her affliction is then repeated. We saw this same sort of repetition in the story of the daughter of Jairus, which is that case represented the age of the girl when she began to menstruate. In this instance, it is the age of the young woman when she is expected to have some healthy fruit hanging from those branches. Notice that the man who took care of the vineyard claimed that he had been looking for fruit for three years, in other words, since the young woman was fifteen.

The tower that fell represents the young woman's back. She has been walking with a slouch. Jesus straightens her back. Then he gives two parables. The first is the familiar parable of the mustard seed, only this time the seed is the base of the woman's backbone, and it grows into the tree of her spine, with the birds (in place of fruit) perched in the branches. The next parable is of the leaven which is mixed with the flour. What is left out of the parable is the result, which is the leaven will make the dough rise and expand, just as the fruit from the fig tree would grow and swell as it ripens.

There is an additional layer, that of the ox or donkey that has its bonds loosened. Both oxen and donkeys are beasts of burden, draught animals that pull heavy loads. This being the case they require a relatively simple collar and harness system. Much as the miracle of Jairus' daughter was a veiled description of a menstrual pad, this might also be pointing towards some sort of early brassiere.

This gives us two sections that deal with issues that a goddess cult would naturally be concerned with. In the previous volume, I dealt with the miracle of the loaves, where I showed that the events took place with two different groups. The first group was likely made up of Hebrew militants, while the second group was associated with the followers of the goddess Venus.

Secrets of the Genealogies

Other signs connect Jesus to the goddess Venus as well. For instance, the genealogy in Matthew is unusual in that, in addition to the males of the line it lists four females, an abbreviated maternal genealogy if you will. Most of these names will be familiar for readers of the previous volumes.

1 A record of the genealogy of Jesus Christ the son of David, the son of Abraham:
2 Abraham was the father of Isaac, Isaac the father of Jacob, Jacob the father of Judah and his brothers,
3 Judah the father of Perez and Zerah, whose mother was Tamar, Perez the father of Hezron, Hezron the father of Ram,
(Mat 1:1-3 NIV)

The first mention is of Tamar, the woman who supposedly pretended to be a prostitute and slept with Judah, fathering Perez and Zerah. The genealogy then follows Perez, whose name means breach, which I claim signified a breach in the bloodline.

5 Salmon the father of Boaz, whose mother was Rahab, Boaz the father of Obed, whose mother was Ruth, Obed the father of Jesse,
(Mat 1:5 NIV)

Here we have two mothers mentioned. The first, Rahab, was the prostitute who helped Joshua to infiltrate Jericho. The second mention is of Ruth, who uncovered the 'feet' of Boaz before becoming his wife.

6 and Jesse the father of King David. David was the father of Solomon, whose mother had been Uriah's wife,
(Mat 1:6 NIV)

Bathsheba: Mother of Solomon

Here, the text neglects to name Uriah's wife, she who slept with David and gave birth to Solomon. Her name was Bathsheba. The name itself is traditionally translated as Daughter of an Oath, but it can just as easily be rendered as Daughter of Seven. As I have shown in earlier volumes, seven is the number associated with the goddess Venus. Here is her story:

2 One evening David got up from his bed and walked around on the roof of the palace. From the roof he saw a woman bathing. The woman was very beautiful,

3 and David sent someone to find out about her. The man said, "Isn't this Bathsheba, the daughter of Eliam and the wife of Uriah the Hittite?"

4 Then David sent messengers to get her. She came to him, and he slept with her. (She had purified herself from her uncleanness.) Then she went back home.

5 The woman conceived and sent word to David, saying, "I am pregnant."

6 So David sent this word to Joab: "Send me Uriah the Hittite." And Joab sent him to David.

7 When Uriah came to him, David asked him how Joab was, how the soldiers were and how the war was going.

8 Then David said to Uriah, "Go down to your house and wash your feet." So Uriah left the palace, and a gift from the king was sent after him.

(2Sa 11:2-8 NIV)

OK, a few points concerning the section above. David sees Bathsheba bathing; he finds out that she is the wife of one of his mighty men, one of his high ranking soldiers. Bathsheba tells David that she is pregnant. David calls Uriah to report to him concerning the war. David then commands him to go to his house and wash his 'feet'. I have already discussed how when the Bible uses the term 'feet' it is often used euphemistically to refer to male genitalia. So David is basically ordering Uriah to go home and have sex with his wife, Bathsheba.

9 But Uriah slept at the entrance to the palace with all his master's servants and did not go down to his house.

10 When David was told, "Uriah did not go home," he asked him, "Haven't you just come from a distance? Why didn't you go home?"

11 Uriah said to David, "The ark and Israel and Judah are staying in tents, and my master Joab and my lord's men are camped in the open fields. How could I go to my house to eat and drink and lie with my wife? As surely as you live, I will not do such a thing!"

12 Then David said to him, "Stay here one more day, and tomorrow I will send you back." So Uriah remained in Jerusalem that day and the next.

13 At David's invitation, he ate and drank with him, and David made him drunk. But in the evening Uriah went out to sleep on his mat among his master's servants; he did not go home.

(2Sa 11:9-13 NIV)

Uriah will not go and sleep with his wife while his men are still on the battlefield. David gets him drunk, but again Uriah will not go home to his wife.

14 In the morning David wrote a letter to Joab and sent it with Uriah.

15 In it he wrote, "Put Uriah in the front line where the fighting is fiercest. Then withdraw from him so he will be struck down and die."

16 So while Joab had the city under siege, he put Uriah at a place where he knew the strongest defenders were.

17 When the men of the city came out and fought against Joab, some of the men in David's army fell; moreover, Uriah the Hittite died.

18 Joab sent David a full account of the battle.

19 He instructed the messenger: "When you have finished giving the king this account of the battle,

20 the king's anger may flare up, and he may ask you, 'Why did you get so close to the city to fight? Didn't you know they would shoot arrows from the wall?

21 Who killed Abimelech son of Jerub-Besheth? Didn't a woman throw an upper millstone on him from the wall, so that he died in Thebez? Why did you get so close to the wall?' If he asks you this, then say to him, 'Also, your servant Uriah the Hittite is dead.'"

22 The messenger set out, and when he arrived he told David everything Joab had sent him to say.

23 The messenger said to David, "The men overpowered us and came out against us in the open, but we drove them back to the entrance to the city gate.

24 Then the archers shot arrows at your servants from the wall, and some of the king's men died. Moreover, your servant Uriah the Hittite is dead."

25 David told the messenger, "Say this to Joab: 'Don't let this upset you; the sword devours one as well as another. Press the attack against the city and destroy it.' Say this to encourage Joab."

26 When Uriah's wife heard that her husband was dead, she mourned for him.

27 After the time of mourning was over, David had her brought to his house, and she became his wife and bore him a son. But the thing David had done displeased the LORD.
(2Sa 11:14-27 NIV)

David then plots to have Uriah killed in battle. Everything goes according to his plan, Uriah dies, and David marries Bathsheba who then bears him a son. But then the prophet Nathan had to come and ruin everything.

2 Samuel 12:1 The LORD sent Nathan to David. When he came to him, he said, "There were two men in a certain town, one rich and the other poor.

2 The rich man had a very large number of sheep and cattle,

3 but the poor man had nothing except one little ewe lamb he had bought. He raised it, and it grew up with him and his children. It shared his food, drank from his cup and even slept in his arms. It was like a daughter to him.

4 "Now a traveler came to the rich man, but the rich man refrained from taking one of his own sheep or cattle to prepare a meal for the traveler who had come to him. Instead, he took the ewe lamb that belonged to the poor man and prepared it for the one who had come to him."

5 David burned with anger against the man and said to Nathan, "As surely as the LORD lives, the man who did this deserves to die!

6 He must pay for that lamb four times over, because he did such a thing and had no pity."
(2Sa 12:1-6 NIV)

Nathan tells David the story of the poor man and his little lamb. David is enraged by the injustice.

7 Then Nathan said to David, "You are the man! This is what the LORD, the God of Israel, says: 'I anointed you king over Israel, and I delivered you from the hand of Saul.

8 I gave your master's house to you, and your master's wives into your arms. I gave you the house of Israel and Judah. And if all this had been too little, I would have given you even more.

9 Why did you despise the word of the LORD by doing what is evil in his eyes? You struck down Uriah the Hittite with the sword and took his wife to be your own. You killed him with the sword of the Ammonites.

10 Now, therefore, the sword will never depart from your house, because you despised me and took the wife of Uriah the Hittite to be your own.'

11 "This is what the LORD says: 'Out of your own household I am going to bring calamity upon you. Before your very eyes I will take your wives and give them to one who is close to you, and he will lie with your wives in broad daylight.

12 You did it in secret, but I will do this thing in broad daylight before all Israel.' "

13 Then David said to Nathan, "I have sinned against the LORD." Nathan replied, "The LORD has taken away your sin. You are not going to die.

14 But because by doing this you have made the enemies of the LORD show utter contempt, the son born to you will die."

(2Sa 12:7-14 NIV)

The Child Must Die

David is cursed. For us, the most crucial aspect of this curse is that his son, mothered by Bathsheba, is to die.

15 After Nathan had gone home, the LORD struck the child that Uriah's wife had borne to David, and he became ill.

16 David pleaded with God for the child. He fasted and went into his house and spent the nights lying on the ground.

17 The elders of his household stood beside him to get him up from the ground, but he refused, and he would not eat any food with them.

18 On the seventh day the child died. David's servants were afraid to tell him that the child was dead, for they thought, "While the child was still living, we spoke to David but he would not listen to us. How can we tell him the child is dead? He may do something desperate."

19 David noticed that his servants were whispering among themselves and he realized the child was dead. "Is the child dead?" he asked. "Yes," they replied, "he is dead."

20 Then David got up from the ground. After he had washed, put on lotions and changed his clothes, he went into the house of the LORD and worshiped. Then he went to his own house, and at his request they served him food, and he ate.

21 His servants asked him, "Why are you acting this way? While the child was alive, you fasted and wept, but now that the child is dead, you get up and eat!"

22 He answered, "While the child was still alive, I fasted and wept. I thought, 'Who knows? The LORD may be gracious to me and let the child live.'

23 But now that he is dead, why should I fast? Can I bring him back again? I will go to him, but he will not return to me."
(2Sa 12:15-23 NIV)

David pleads with God for his son's life. He fasts and sleeps on the ground. He refused to eat or to get up off of the ground. Then, once he is informed that his son has died, he gets up, washes, and perfumes himself, dresses, and eats. The servants are confused by his behavior. While the child was alive, he fasted and wept, but now that he is dead he eats and dresses himself. David explains away this paradox, but perhaps there is more here than is apparent at first glance.

Let us go back to the beginning when David first saw Bathsheba. He saw her and then he immediately wanted her. Sometime after they had sex, she informed him that she was pregnant. It then became David's problem that Bathsheba was pregnant. Obviously, we are meant to understand that when Bathsheba discovered that she was pregnant, she was aware that the timing of her pregnancy would make it obvious to her husband Uriah that she had been unfaithful.

So she communicated this to David who then took the necessary steps to conceal Bathsheba's adultery.

Now, however, let us consider the possibility that Bathsheba was a follower of the goddess Venus and that she was a sacred prostitute. We have seen how this group could interfere with and manipulate the patriarchal bloodlines. Most importantly, their actions are veiled, with the high-priestesses the unseen puppet-masters obscured by shadow.

Perhaps David was merely a puppet dancing on hidden strings. He sees a beautiful woman and instantly desires her. Maybe that was her intention. Probably Bathsheba was already pregnant when David first saw her and David seeing her was part of her plan. But not hers alone, instead it was the work of an entire network of goddess worshipers, who had long waited for just such an opportunity. Bathsheba carried within her womb a child specifically bred to breach the bloodline. David was seduced. Uriah was called back to meet with David and the followers of the goddess made sure that he would not visit his wife as David had ordered. For if David had been successful, then Bathsheba would have remained married to Uriah, who would remain unaware that the child was not his. So it seems likely that the followers of the goddess employed every means possible to remind Uriah of his duty to his men and to keep him from returning his wife. Eventually, David saw himself as having no choice other than having Uriah killed. Then he found himself basically having to marry Bathsheba with the child becoming his heir.

Reading between the lines, it seems that Nathan realized what Bathsheba and the followers of the goddess were up to and informed David what must be done. The child that Bathsheba initially gave birth to was no more David's than it was Uriah's. This helps to explain David's behavior. He fasted and prayed for God to kill the child because it was not his. Once the child had died, he could rule in peace without fear that another man's son would inherit his kingdom. Even so, the goddess's breeding program ensured that half of Solomon's genes came from Bathsheba, Daughter of Seven.

With that bit of business out of the way, we shall now return to the genealogy of Jesus which concludes with the following:

16 and Jacob the father of Joseph, the husband of Mary, of whom was born Jesus, who is called Christ.

(Mat 1:16 NIV)

Here we see once again the mother being mentioned: Tamar, Rahab, Ruth, Bathsheba, and Mary. Five mothers mentioned on a single bloodline. And yet out of the two genealogies provided for Jesus, it is Luke's which is thought to document the bloodline of Mary.

The Genealogy from Matthew

First, we will look a little closer at Matthew's list, which is divided into three groups of fourteen each.

The first fourteen are from Abraham to David.

Abraham
Isaac
Jacob
Judah and Tamar
Perez
Hezron
Ram
Aminadab
Nahshon
Salmon and Rachab
Boaz and Ruth
Obed
Jesse
David and Bathsheba

Figure 3. First fourteen entries from Matthew's genealogy.

The second list of fourteen runs from Solomon to Jeconiah.

Solomon
Rehoboam
Abijah
Asa
Jehoshaphat
Jehoram
Ahaziah
Jotham
Ahaz
Hezekiah
Manasseh
Amon
Josiah
Jeconiah

Figure 4. Second series of fourteen entries from Matthew's genealogy.

The third runs from Shealtiel to Jesus. It is during this third section after Zerubbabel that the list moves from known names to unknown names, until finally returning to Joseph and Jesus. Actually, there are only thirteen in the last group, rather than fourteen, unless Mary is included in the list. The Matthew list has just nine names in total which refer to unknown individuals.

<u>Shealtiel</u>
<u>Zerubbabel</u>
Abiud
Eliakim
Azor
Zadok
Achim
Eliud
Eleazar
Matthan
Jacob
<u>Joseph</u>
<u>Mary</u>
<u>Jesus</u>

Figure 5. Third series of fourteen entries from Matthew's genealogy.

The Genealogy from Luke

Turning now to Luke's genealogy we find that it goes all the way back to God.

God
Adam
Seth
Enos
Cainan
Maleleel
Jared
Enoch
Mathusala
Lamech
Noah
Shem
Arphaxad
Cainan
Sala
Heber
Phalec
Ragau
Saruch
Nachor
Thara

Figure 6. The earliest part of Luke's genealogy.

Matthew's genealogy	Luke's genealogy
Abraham	Abraham
Isaac	Isaac
Jacob	Jacob
Judah and Tamar	Juda
Perez	Phares
Hezron	Esrom
Ram	Aram
Aminadab	Aminadab
Nahshon	Naasson
Salmon and Rachab	Salmon
Boaz and Ruth	Boaz
Obed	Obed
Jesse	Jesse
David and Bathsheba	David

Figure 7. Comparison of Matthew and Luke's genealogy from Abraham to David.

Then from Abraham to David, Luke synchronizes perfectly with Mathew. However, once we get to Nathan, who is David and Bathsheba's third son, rather than Solomon, David and Bathsheba's more famous second son, we see that Luke has deviated almost entirely from Matthew.

Nathan	
Mattatha	Matthew
Menan	
Melea	
Eliakim	Eliakim
Jonam	John
Joseph	Joseph
Judah	Judah
Simeon	Simeon
Levi	Levi
Matthat	Matthew
Jorim	
Eliezer	
Jose	Joseph
Er	
Elmodam	
Cosam	
Addi	
Melchi	Melchi
Neri	
Salathiel	

Figure 8. Luke's genealogy from Nathan to Salathiel with variations identified.

From Solomon to Jeconiah, the sequence in Matthew followed the Davidic royal line with a few omissions. Luke, on the other hand, lists nineteen unknown individuals beginning after Nathan, until we reach Shealtiel and Zerubbabel, which are the only two names shared between Matthew and Luke in this section of the genealogies. Following these two known names, Luke continues with another eighteen unknown individuals until we finally arrive at Joseph.

Zorobabel	
Rhesa	
Joannan	John
Juda	Judah
Joseph	Joseph
Semei	Simeon
Mattathias	Matthew
Maath	
Nagge	
Esli	
Naum	
Amos	
Mattathias	Matthew
Joseph	Joseph
Jannai	
Melchi	Melchi
Levi	Levi
Matthat	Matthew
Heli	Eliakim
Joseph	Joseph
Jesus	

Figure 9. Luke's genealogy from Zorobabel to Jesus with variations identified.

Strangely enough, these thirty-seven unknown individuals often have the same name or variants of the same name. There are two men named Mattathias, but Mattatha and Matthat are just different forms of the same name, Matthew. There are three Josephs, four if we count Mary's husband. There is also one Jose which is also just another form of Joseph. There are two Levis. There are both Judah and Juda, which are forms the same name. Jonam and Joannan are different forms of the name John. There are also two with the name Melchi, which means king. There is also one Simeon and one Semei which is another form of Simeon. Finally, we have the somewhat obscure pair of Eliakim and Heli, which are again alternative forms of the same name. [1]

If we assign all of the names to their primary forms, we have five of Matthew, five of Joseph, two of Levi, two of Judah, two of John, two of Simeon, two of Melchi, and two of Eliakim. These names are distributed evenly between the two halves of the list beginning with the section running from Mattatha to Neri. The second section runs from Rhesa to Joseph. Each section contains nineteen entries and the following pattern. When there are two entries of the same name, they are split between the two sections. When there are five entries of the same name, the entries are divided with two in the first section and three in the second.

If we study the two lists above from Luke, it soon becomes evident that this is no simple genealogy. Parents are not going to name their sons according to some predetermined sequence of names. Notice the series in the first sequence above running Jonam (John), Joseph, Judah, Simeon, Levi, Matthat (Matthew) and then from the second section, the sequence Joannan (John), Juda (Judah), Joseph, Semei (Simeon), Mattathias (Matthew). The second is a simple variation of the first.

What we have here are eight specific lines, specifically bred and maintained over centuries, if not millennia. Each line has some quality or feature that has been isolated and honed over generations until it is as pure an expression of that characteristic directed breeding and human genetics will allow. The other names represent breeder material of a less refined nature, likely from candidates of exceptional qualities that were added to fine-tune the genetic concoction they were attempting to breed. Also, there are those times when the breeders fail to follow the plan resulting in wild strains intermixed with the pure.

The first section shows the breeding sequence using the seed of Nathan, the third of David's four sons with Bathsheba. It is too early in our study to determine what the line of Matthew's specific quality

---

[1] An argument could be made that the name Jannai is a form of John and that Maath is a form of Matthew. However, I am allowing for the more conservative reading as found in Strong's Concordance and others which assumes these names are based on Hebrew roots. That being the case, the meaning of Jannai is 'to oppress, suppress, treat violently, maltreat, vex, do wrong,' while the meaning of Maath is simply 'small.'

is, but to it was then added a wild stain with the label Menan. This name's meaning is "soothsayer", so it isn't too much of a leap of logic to suppose that this indicated that the contributor of the genetic material was supposedly able to see the future. The next name means "my dear friend/object of care" which perhaps indicates that genetic material came from someone the offspring of the soothsayer loved rather than the individual needed for the sequence. After this, the next seven generations are from the eight pure strains, minus Melchi. Then comes a Jorim "whom Jehovah has exalted" and an Eliezar "God is his help," which I suppose are self-explanatory labels. Then, there is another injection of the Joseph strain. Next is a wild strain labeled Er "watchful" which might be interpreted as indicating this genetic material is coming from a Watcher, a fallen angel. This is also the name of Judah's eldest son with Canaanite wife, Shuah. According to the book of Genesis:

7 And Er, Judah's firstborn, was wicked in the sight of the LORD; and the LORD slew him.
(Gen 38:7 KJV)

Perhaps the reason that Er, the son of Judah, was evil in the eyes of the Lord was that his real father was a Watcher who had either tricked or seduced Shuah, Judah's Canaanite wife. The name Er might indicate someone carrying Watcher blood.

Returning to the sequence next is Elmodam meaning "measure" perhaps indicating someone good at mathematics. Then Cosam "divining" indicating the DNA of another fortune teller was added to the mix. The name Addi "ornament" probably indicates that the next individual was chosen for their physical attractiveness. Finally, the last of the eight pure strains Mechi is introduced. This name means "king" and is part of the name of Melchizedek, who was the king of Salem and the priest of the Most High written of in Genesis chapter 14. Next is a wild strain labeled Neri "Jehovah is my lamp."

From here the list goes above ground to Shealtiel and his son Zerubbabel as referred to in Matthew's list. We know nothing about Shealtiel beyond his name and the only reason we know Shealtiel is Zerubbabel's father is because Zerubbabel is identified as "Zerubbabel son of Shealtiel" in the Books of Ezra and Nehemiah. This apparently means this carefully cultivated bloodline moved back into history in the person of Zerubbabel, whose name means "the one sown of Babylon" or perhaps "the seed of Babylon." Zerubbabel led the first group of Jews out of Babylonian captivity. He also laid the foundation of the Second Temple in Jerusalem.

What this apparently indicates is that this secret breeding project went through nineteen generations after going underground following Nathan and then resurfaced when it breached the royal bloodline to produce a leader that would lead the people out of Babylon. Then the genetic material of Zerubbabel served as the starting point for the next nineteen generation underground breeding sequence that surfaced again with Jesus.

This second sequence is much like the first, though instead of there being two Matthews and Josephs there are now three of each. It is not yet possible to determine precisely what sort of quality the name Matthew indicates. Most of the names belonged to famous personages found in the books of the Old Testament, and it is likely that their inclusion means that these bloodlines originated with those named. Almost all of those named had some connection to sacred prostitution.

Judah

Judah was the name of the fourth son of Jacob and Leah. His two older full brothers were Simeon and Levi. Judah, as you will recall from volume four, was the man who supposedly had sex with Tamar when she was allegedly posing as a temple prostitute. As you will remember, I read the text as indicating that Judah actually did not have sex with Tamar, he was tricked into believing he had done so by the followers of the goddess Venus so that the children Tamar carried might breach the bloodline of the patriarchs. Looking at the genealogy above, it is clear that this breach was successful as King David is a descendant of Tamar's son Perez/Phares. In his blessing, Jacob proclaims the following concerning Judah:

8 "Judah, your brothers will praise you; your hand will be on the neck of your enemies; your father's sons will bow down to you.
9 You are a lion's cub, O Judah; you return from the prey, my son. Like a lion he crouches and lies down, like a lioness--who dares to rouse him?

10 The scepter will not depart from Judah, nor the ruler's staff from between his feet, until he comes to whom it belongs and the obedience of the nations is his.

11 He will tether his donkey to a vine, his colt to the choicest branch; he will wash his garments in wine, his robes in the blood of grapes.

12 His eyes will be darker than wine, his teeth whiter than milk. (Gen 49:8-12 NIV)

Simeon and Levi

The bloodline of Judah was somewhat obliquely associated with sacred prostitution. Judah's older brothers Simeon and Levi were connected to the theme of prostitution because when their sister Dinah was raped by a Canaanite named Shechem, they tricked all of the men of his city to get circumcised after which Simeon and Levi slaughtered the men in their weakened condition and sacked the city. Their justification was that Shechem had treated their sister Dinah like a prostitute. Both were later cursed by their father Jacob and told that their descendants would become divided and scattered.

5 Simeon and Levi are brothers-- their swords are weapons of violence.

6 Let me not enter their council, let me not join their assembly, for they have killed men in their anger and hamstrung oxen as they pleased.

7 Cursed be their anger, so fierce, and their fury, so cruel! I will scatter them in Jacob and disperse them in Israel.

(Gen 49:5-7 NIV)

So the bloodlines of both Levi and Simeon were cursed, yet it seems that for whatever reason the followers of the goddess sought to preserve them. In time the Levites returned to significance through Aaron and Moses and became the bloodline of the priesthood. Readers of volume four will recall that fingerprints of the followers of the goddess were all over Moses' birth. Moses set up the tribe of Levites as the hereditary line of priests. So it was no doubt easier to maintain the bloodline of Levi than it was of Simeon.

Joseph

Next, we come to Joseph, whose story was thoroughly examined in the previous volume. He was Jacob's favorite son, who was sold into slavery in Egypt by his brothers and who soon rose in importance to become vizier of Egypt. More importantly, his birth seemed to be the product of a generations-long breeding project by the goddess religion to create a man capable of both successfully interpreting dreams and managing a kingdom's food supply well enough to survive seven years of famine.

22 "Joseph is a fruitful vine, a fruitful vine near a spring, whose branches climb over a wall.
23 With bitterness archers attacked him; they shot at him with hostility.
24 But his bow remained steady, his strong arms stayed limber, because of the hand of the Mighty One of Jacob, because of the Shepherd, the Rock of Israel,
25 because of your father's God, who helps you, because of the Almighty, who blesses you with blessings of the heavens above, blessings of the deep that lies below, blessings of the breast and womb.
26 Your father's blessings are greater than the blessings of the ancient mountains, than the bounty of the age-old hills. Let all these rest on the head of Joseph, on the brow of the prince among his brothers.
(Gen 49:22-26 NIV)

Notice that while Joseph has no apparent connection to sacred prostitution beyond being the result of its breeding project, Jacob does include a rather obvious nod to the goddess in his blessing: *"blessings of the deep that lies below, blessings of the breast and womb."*

Jonathan

Next, we come to John. In the Old Testament, there are as many as eleven different individuals named Jonathan. Still, the most famous and most likely referent is the eldest son of King Saul. To understand this man we must first learn his story.

It is a story of a slaughter.

1 Samuel 13:1 Saul was thirty years old when he became king, and he reigned over Israel forty-two years.

2 Saul chose three thousand men from Israel; two thousand were with him at Micmash and in the hill country of Bethel, and a thousand were with Jonathan at Gibeah in Benjamin. The rest of the men he sent back to their homes.

3 Jonathan attacked the Philistine outpost at Geba, and the Philistines heard about it. Then Saul had the trumpet blown throughout the land and said, "Let the Hebrews hear!"

4 So all Israel heard the news: "Saul has attacked the Philistine outpost, and now Israel has become a stench to the Philistines." And the people were summoned to join Saul at Gilgal.

5 The Philistines assembled to fight Israel, with three thousand chariots, six thousand charioteers, and soldiers as numerous as the sand on the seashore. They went up and camped at Micmash, east of Beth Aven.

6 When the men of Israel saw that their situation was critical and that their army was hard pressed, they hid in caves and thickets, among the rocks, and in pits and cisterns.

7 Some Hebrews even crossed the Jordan to the land of Gad and Gilead. Saul remained at Gilgal, and all the troops with him were quaking with fear.

8 He waited seven days, the time set by Samuel; but Samuel did not come to Gilgal, and Saul's men began to scatter.

9 So he said, "Bring me the burnt offering and the fellowship offerings." And Saul offered up the burnt offering.

10 Just as he finished making the offering, Samuel arrived, and Saul went out to greet him.

11 "What have you done?" asked Samuel. Saul replied, "When I saw that the men were scattering, and that you did not come at the set time, and that the Philistines were assembling at Micmash,

12 I thought, 'Now the Philistines will come down against me at Gilgal, and I have not sought the LORD's favor.' So I felt compelled to offer the burnt offering."

13 "You acted foolishly," Samuel said. "You have not kept the command the LORD your God gave you; if you had, he would have established your kingdom over Israel for all time.

14 But now your kingdom will not endure; the LORD has sought out a man after his own heart and appointed him leader of his people, because you have not kept the LORD's command."

15 Then Samuel left Gilgal and went up to Gibeah in Benjamin, and Saul counted the men who were with him. They numbered about six hundred.

16 Saul and his son Jonathan and the men with them were staying in Gibeah in Benjamin, while the Philistines camped at Micmash.

17 Raiding parties went out from the Philistine camp in three detachments. One turned toward Ophrah in the vicinity of Shual,

18 another toward Beth Horon, and the third toward the borderland overlooking the Valley of Zeboim facing the desert.

19 Not a blacksmith could be found in the whole land of Israel, because the Philistines had said, "Otherwise the Hebrews will make swords or spears!"

20 So all Israel went down to the Philistines to have their plowshares, mattocks, axes and sickles sharpened.

21 The price was two thirds of a shekel for sharpening plowshares and mattocks, and a third of a shekel for sharpening forks and axes and for repointing goads.

22 So on the day of the battle not a soldier with Saul and Jonathan had a sword or spear in his hand; only Saul and his son Jonathan had them.

23 Now a detachment of Philistines had gone out to the pass at Micmash.
(1Sa 13:1-23 NIV)

Saul attacked the Philistines expected that Samuel would come with reinforcements. Instead, Samuel said that God had deserted Saul and so Samuel must then desert him as well. Saul, Jonathan and about six hundred men remained to defend against the tens of thousands of Philistine soldiers. The Philistines had removed all of the blacksmiths from the land so that no weapons could be forged which resulted in the men being armed with farming tools, rather than swords or spears.

1 Samuel 14:1 One day Jonathan son of Saul said to the young man bearing his armor, "Come, let's go over to the Philistine outpost on the other side." But he did not tell his father.

2 Saul was staying on the outskirts of Gibeah under a pomegranate tree in Migron. With him were about six hundred men,

*3 among whom was Ahijah, who was wearing an **ephod**. He was a son of Ichabod's brother Ahitub son of Phinehas, the son of Eli, the LORD's priest in Shiloh. No one was aware that Jonathan had left.*

4 On each side of the pass that Jonathan intended to cross to reach the Philistine outpost was a cliff; one was called Bozez, and the other Seneh.

5 One cliff stood to the north toward Micmash, the other to the south toward Geba.

6 Jonathan said to his young armor-bearer, "Come, let's go over to the outpost of those uncircumcised fellows. Perhaps the LORD will act in our behalf. Nothing can hinder the LORD from saving, whether by many or by few."

7 "Do all that you have in mind," his armor-bearer said. "Go ahead; I am with you heart and soul."

8 Jonathan said, "Come, then; we will cross over toward the men and let them see us.

9 If they say to us, 'Wait there until we come to you,' we will stay where we are and not go up to them.

10 But if they say, 'Come up to us,' we will climb up, because that will be our sign that the LORD has given them into our hands."

11 So both of them showed themselves to the Philistine outpost. "Look!" said the Philistines. "The Hebrews are crawling out of the holes they were hiding in."

12 The men of the outpost shouted to Jonathan and his armor-bearer, "Come up to us and we'll teach you a lesson." So Jonathan said to his armor-bearer, "Climb up after me; the LORD has given them into the hand of Israel."

13 Jonathan climbed up, using his hands and feet, with his armor-bearer right behind him. The Philistines fell before Jonathan, and his armor-bearer followed and killed behind him.

14 In that first attack Jonathan and his armor-bearer killed some twenty men in an area of about half an acre.

15 Then panic struck the whole army--those in the camp and field, and those in the outposts and raiding parties--and the ground shook. It was a panic sent by God.

16 Saul's lookouts at Gibeah in Benjamin saw the army melting away in all directions.

17 Then Saul said to the men who were with him, "Muster the forces and see who has left us." When they did, it was Jonathan and his armor-bearer who were not there.

18 Saul said to Ahijah, "Bring the ark of God." (At that time it was with the Israelites.)

19 While Saul was talking to the priest, the tumult in the Philistine camp increased more and more. So Saul said to the priest, "Withdraw your hand."

20 Then Saul and all his men assembled and went to the battle. They found the Philistines in total confusion, striking each other with their swords.

21 Those Hebrews who had previously been with the Philistines and had gone up with them to their camp went over to the Israelites who were with Saul and Jonathan.

22 When all the Israelites who had hidden in the hill country of Ephraim heard that the Philistines were on the run, they joined the battle in hot pursuit.

23 So the LORD rescued Israel that day, and the battle moved on beyond Beth Aven.

(1Sa 14:1-23 NIV)

Readers of the previous volume will note the similarity to Gideon's victory over the Midianite army:

19 Gideon and the hundred men with him reached the edge of the camp at the beginning of the middle watch, just after they had changed the guard. They blew their trumpets and broke the jars that were in their hands.

20 The three companies blew the trumpets and smashed the jars. Grasping the torches in their left hands and holding in their right hands the trumpets they were to blow, they shouted, "A sword for the LORD and for Gideon!"

21 While each man held his position around the camp, all the Midianites ran, crying out as they fled.

22 When the three hundred trumpets sounded, the LORD caused the men throughout the camp to turn on each other with their swords.

(Jdg 7:19-22 NIV)

Returning to Jonathan's story, we find another clue binding these two events:

*24 Now the men of Israel were in distress that day, because
Saul had bound the people under an oath, saying, "Cursed be any
man who eats food before evening comes, before I have avenged
myself on my enemies!" So none of the troops tasted food.*

*25 The entire army entered the woods, and there was honey on
the ground.*

*26 When they went into the woods, they saw the honey oozing
out, yet no one put his hand to his mouth, because they feared the
oath.*

*27 But Jonathan had not heard that his father had bound the
people with the oath, so he reached out the end of the staff that was
in his hand and dipped it into the honeycomb. He raised his hand to
his mouth, and his eyes brightened.*

*28 Then one of the soldiers told him, "Your father bound the
army under a strict oath, saying, 'Cursed be any man who eats food
today!' That is why the men are faint."*

*29 Jonathan said, "My father has made trouble for the country.
See how my eyes brightened when I tasted a little of this honey.*

*30 How much better it would have been if the men had eaten
today some of the plunder they took from their enemies. Would not
the slaughter of the Philistines have been even greater?"*
(1Sa 14:24-30 NIV)

Eat No Tainted Food

Saul forbade any of his people to eat any food. Why? The food
was likely infected with ergot-infected grain. This explains how
Jonathan's small attack caused the entire army to panic. The
Philistines saw the Hebrews crawling out of the holes they were
hiding in even when there weren't any Hebrews around, but just
other hallucinating Philistines.

*36 Saul said, "Let us go down after the Philistines by night and
plunder them till dawn, and let us not leave one of them alive." "Do
whatever seems best to you," they replied. But the priest said, "Let us
inquire of God here."*

*37 So Saul asked God, "Shall I go down after the Philistines?
Will you give them into Israel's hand?" But God did not answer him
that day.*

38 Saul therefore said, "Come here, all you who are leaders of the army, and let us find out what sin has been committed today.

39 As surely as the LORD who rescues Israel lives, even if it lies with my son Jonathan, he must die." But not one of the men said a word.

40 Saul then said to all the Israelites, "You stand over there; I and Jonathan my son will stand over here." "Do what seems best to you," the men replied.

41 Then Saul prayed to the LORD, the God of Israel, "Give me the right answer." And Jonathan and Saul were taken by lot, and the men were cleared.

42 Saul said, "Cast the lot between me and Jonathan my son." And Jonathan was taken.

43 Then Saul said to Jonathan, "Tell me what you have done." So Jonathan told him, "I merely tasted a little honey with the end of my staff. And now must I die?"

44 Saul said, "May God deal with me, be it ever so severely, if you do not die, Jonathan."

45 But the men said to Saul, "Should Jonathan die--he who has brought about this great deliverance in Israel? Never! As surely as the LORD lives, not a hair of his head will fall to the ground, for he did this today with God's help." So the men rescued Jonathan, and he was not put to death.

46 Then Saul stopped pursuing the Philistines, and they withdrew to their own land.

(1Sa 14:36-46 NIV)

In the above section, we have an example of Saul inquiring of God and then using the drawing of lots to determine God's answer. Notice above in First Samuel 14:3 how Ahijah, one of the six hundred men with Saul, is described as wearing an ephod. This is the breastplate worn by the high priest and was used with the mysterious Urim and Thummim to determine God's will. I suspect that initially the system worked similarly if not identically to the I Ching before devolving to being a system for choosing between two groups, one being innocent, the other guilty. Also, I suspect that the arrangement of the jewels on the breastplate could be arranged to covertly convey a message to those in the audience of the ritual capable of decoding it.

To Drink Honey from the End of a Staff

You may have noticed the somewhat overt sexual symbolism of Jonathan claiming, "I merely tasted a little honey with the end of my staff. And now must I die?" Drinking honey from the end of a staff can be read in a couple of ways. Much like the manner in which the identity of the fruit of knowledge was concealed behind a sexual reading, it seems that the same mechanism is employed with Jonathan, whose relationship with David could be read as having homosexual undertones.

1 Samuel 18:1 After David had finished talking with Saul, Jonathan became one in spirit with David, and he loved him as himself.

2 From that day Saul kept David with him and did not let him return to his father's house.

3 And Jonathan made a covenant with David because he loved him as himself.

4 Jonathan took off the robe he was wearing and gave it to David, along with his tunic, and even his sword, his bow and his belt.

5 Whatever Saul sent him to do, David did it so successfully that Saul gave him a high rank in the army. This pleased all the people, and Saul's officers as well.

6 When the men were returning home after David had killed the Philistine, the women came out from all the towns of Israel to meet King Saul with singing and dancing, with joyful songs and with tambourines and lutes.

7 As they danced, they sang: "Saul has slain his thousands, and David his tens of thousands."

8 Saul was very angry; this refrain galled him. "They have credited David with tens of thousands," he thought, "but me with only thousands. What more can he get but the kingdom?"

9 And from that time on Saul kept a jealous eye on David.

10 The next day an evil spirit from God came forcefully upon Saul. He was prophesying in his house, while David was playing the harp, as he usually did. Saul had a spear in his hand

11 and he hurled it, saying to himself, "I'll pin David to the wall." But David eluded him twice.

12 Saul was afraid of David, because the LORD was with David but had left Saul.

13 So he sent David away from him and gave him command over a thousand men, and David led the troops in their campaigns. (1Sa 18:1-13 NIV)

Strangely, even Saul attacking David with a spear, saying to himself, "I will pin David to the wall," has some rather overt homosexual symbolism.

14 In everything he did he had great success, because the LORD was with him.

15 When Saul saw how successful he was, he was afraid of him.

16 But all Israel and Judah loved David, because he led them in their campaigns.

17 Saul said to David, "Here is my older daughter Merab. I will give her to you in marriage; only serve me bravely and fight the battles of the LORD." For Saul said to himself, "I will not raise a hand against him. Let the Philistines do that!"

18 But David said to Saul, "Who am I, and what is my family or my father's clan in Israel, that I should become the king's son-in-law?"

19 So when the time came for Merab, Saul's daughter, to be given to David, she was given in marriage to Adriel of Meholah.

20 Now Saul's daughter Michal was in love with David, and when they told Saul about it, he was pleased.

21 "I will give her to him," he thought, "so that she may be a snare to him and so that the hand of the Philistines may be against him." So Saul said to David, "Now you have a second opportunity to become my son-in-law."

22 Then Saul ordered his attendants: "Speak to David privately and say, 'Look, the king is pleased with you, and his attendants all like you; now become his son-in-law.'"

23 They repeated these words to David. But David said, "Do you think it is a small matter to become the king's son-in-law? I'm only a poor man and little known."

24 When Saul's servants told him what David had said,

25 Saul replied, "Say to David, 'The king wants no other price for the bride than a hundred Philistine foreskins, to take revenge on his enemies.'" Saul's plan was to have David fall by the hands of the Philistines.

26 When the attendants told David these things, he was pleased to become the king's son-in-law. So before the allotted time elapsed,

27 David and his men went out and killed two hundred Philistines. He brought their foreskins and presented the full number to the king so that he might become the king's son-in-law. Then Saul gave him his daughter Michal in marriage.

28 When Saul realized that the LORD was with David and that his daughter Michal loved David,

29 Saul became still more afraid of him, and he remained his enemy the rest of his days.

30 The Philistine commanders continued to go out to battle, and as often as they did, David met with more success than the rest of Saul's officers, and his name became well known.

(1Sa 18:14-30 NIV)

Saul tries to bring David under his control by marrying him off to his daughter. David shows that he is too humble, who is he to marry the daughter of a king? Saul takes note and with the offer of his second daughter Saul names a price so that David might die to try to prove himself worthy, the foreskins of a hundred Philistines. David delivers double that number, and after Saul marries his daughter to David, he fears him more than ever. But foreskins, Saul are you being serious right now?

1 Samuel 19:1 Saul told his son Jonathan and all the attendants to kill David. But Jonathan was very fond of David

2 and warned him, "My father Saul is looking for a chance to kill you. Be on your guard tomorrow morning; go into hiding and stay there.

3 I will go out and stand with my father in the field where you are. I'll speak to him about you and will tell you what I find out."

4 Jonathan spoke well of David to Saul his father and said to him, "Let not the king do wrong to his servant David; he has not wronged you, and what he has done has benefited you greatly.

5 He took his life in his hands when he killed the Philistine. The LORD won a great victory for all Israel, and you saw it and were glad. Why then would you do wrong to an innocent man like David by killing him for no reason?"

6 Saul listened to Jonathan and took this oath: "As surely as the LORD lives, David will not be put to death."

7 So Jonathan called David and told him the whole conversation. He brought him to Saul, and David was with Saul as before.

8 Once more war broke out, and David went out and fought the Philistines. He struck them with such force that they fled before him.

9 But an evil spirit from the LORD came upon Saul as he was sitting in his house with his spear in his hand. While David was playing the harp,

10 Saul tried to pin him to the wall with his spear, but David eluded him as Saul drove the spear into the wall. That night David made good his escape.

(1Sa 19:1-10 NIV)

The next chapter begins just like the last, with the David, Jonathan, and Saul triangle ending with Saul once again trying to nail David against the wall with his spear. Then just as before, the second section of the chapter deals with David and his wife.

11 Saul sent men to David's house to watch it and to kill him in the morning. But Michal, David's wife, warned him, "If you don't run for your life tonight, tomorrow you'll be killed."

12 So Michal let David down through a window, and he fled and escaped.

13 Then Michal took an idol and laid it on the bed, covering it with a garment and putting some goats' hair at the head.

14 When Saul sent the men to capture David, Michal said, "He is ill."

15 Then Saul sent the men back to see David and told them, "Bring him up to me in his bed so that I may kill him."

16 But when the men entered, there was the idol in the bed, and at the head was some goats' hair.

17 Saul said to Michal, "Why did you deceive me like this and send my enemy away so that he escaped?" Michal told him, "He said to me, 'Let me get away. Why should I kill you?'"

(1Sa 19:11-17 NIV)

However, this time, the chapter has a third section that reads like some psychedelic sixties comedy where everyone who arrives at a specific location gets fed a blistering dose of ergot-infected grain.

18 When David had fled and made his escape, he went to Samuel at Ramah and told him all that Saul had done to him. Then he and Samuel went to Naioth and stayed there.

19 Word came to Saul: "David is in Naioth at Ramah";

20 so he sent men to capture him. But when they saw a group of prophets prophesying, with Samuel standing there as their leader, the Spirit of God came upon Saul's men and they also prophesied.

21 Saul was told about it, and he sent more men, and they prophesied too. Saul sent men a third time, and they also prophesied.

22 Finally, he himself left for Ramah and went to the great cistern at Secu. And he asked, "Where are Samuel and David?" "Over in Naioth at Ramah," they said.

23 So Saul went to Naioth at Ramah. But the Spirit of God came even upon him, and he walked along prophesying until he came to Naioth.

24 He stripped off his robes and also prophesied in Samuel's presence. He lay that way all that day and night. This is why people say, "Is Saul also among the prophets?"

(1Sa 19:18-1 NIV)

After the event above, we are able to create a time-line concerning David gaining knowledge of the secret of the ergot-infected grain. First Jonathan probably told David about how he and his armor-bearer routed the Palestine army and how Saul forbade anyone to eat during the day. Once Saul became king he must have gained the secret of the bread and immediately used it in his first battle as king. After David received this information, he went to the last of the Judges, Samuel, who was the leader of the people before Saul. Samuel then took David to Naioth at Ramah, where everyone who went there was apparently exposed to the ergot-infected grain. In chapter twenty one, David finally goes to Ahimelech the priest who gives David and his men the sacred loaves.

For now, let us go back to when David manages to escape from Saul and meets up with Jonathan:

1 Samuel 20:1 Then David fled from Naioth at Ramah and went to Jonathan and asked, "What have I done? What is my crime? How have I wronged your father, that he is trying to take my life?"

2 "Never!" Jonathan replied. "You are not going to die! Look, my father doesn't do anything, great or small, without confiding in me. Why would he hide this from me? It's not so!"

3 But David took an oath and said, "Your father knows very well that I have found favor in your eyes, and he has said to himself, 'Jonathan must not know this or he will be grieved.' Yet as surely as the LORD lives and as you live, there is only a step between me and death."

4 Jonathan said to David, "Whatever you want me to do, I'll do for you."

5 So David said, "Look, tomorrow is the New Moon festival, and I am supposed to dine with the king; but let me go and hide in the field until the evening of the day after tomorrow.

6 If your father misses me at all, tell him, 'David earnestly asked my permission to hurry to Bethlehem, his hometown, because an annual sacrifice is being made there for his whole clan.'

7 If he says, 'Very well,' then your servant is safe. But if he loses his temper, you can be sure that he is determined to harm me.

8 As for you, show kindness to your servant, for you have brought him into a covenant with you before the LORD. If I am guilty, then kill me yourself! Why hand me over to your father?"

9 "Never!" Jonathan said. "If I had the least inkling that my father was determined to harm you, wouldn't I tell you?"

10 David asked, "Who will tell me if your father answers you harshly?"

11 "Come," Jonathan said, "let's go out into the field." So they went there together.

12 Then Jonathan said to David: "By the LORD, the God of Israel, I will surely sound out my father by this time the day after tomorrow! If he is favorably disposed toward you, will I not send you word and let you know?

13 But if my father is inclined to harm you, may the LORD deal with me, be it ever so severely, if I do not let you know and send you away safely. May the LORD be with you as he has been with my father.

14 But show me unfailing kindness like that of the LORD as long as I live, so that I may not be killed,

15 and do not ever cut off your kindness from my family--not even when the LORD has cut off every one of David's enemies from the face of the earth."

16 So Jonathan made a covenant with the house of David, saying, "May the LORD call David's enemies to account."

17 And Jonathan had David reaffirm his oath out of love for him, because he loved him as he loved himself.

18 Then Jonathan said to David: "Tomorrow is the New Moon festival. You will be missed, because your seat will be empty.

19 The day after tomorrow, toward evening, go to the place where you hid when this trouble began, and wait by the stone Ezel.

20 I will shoot three arrows to the side of it, as though I were shooting at a target.

21 Then I will send a boy and say, 'Go, find the arrows.' If I say to him, 'Look, the arrows are on this side of you; bring them here,' then come, because, as surely as the LORD lives, you are safe; there is no danger.

22 But if I say to the boy, 'Look, the arrows are beyond you,' then you must go, because the LORD has sent you away.

23 And about the matter you and I discussed--remember, the LORD is witness between you and me forever."

(1Sa 20:1-23 NIV)

So, the stage is set. Not that the outcome is ever in doubt. Saul has hardly been reasonable up to now.

24 So David hid in the field, and when the New Moon festival came, the king sat down to eat.

25 He sat in his customary place by the wall, opposite Jonathan, and Abner sat next to Saul, but David's place was empty.

26 Saul said nothing that day, for he thought, "Something must have happened to David to make him ceremonially unclean--surely he is unclean."

27 But the next day, the second day of the month, David's place was empty again. Then Saul said to his son Jonathan, "Why hasn't the son of Jesse come to the meal, either yesterday or today?"

28 Jonathan answered, "David earnestly asked me for permission to go to Bethlehem.

29 He said, 'Let me go, because our family is observing a sacrifice in the town and my brother has ordered me to be there. If I have found favor in your eyes, let me get away to see my brothers.' That is why he has not come to the king's table."

30 Saul's anger flared up at Jonathan and he said to him, "You son of a perverse and rebellious woman! Don't I know that you have sided with the son of Jesse to your own shame and to the shame of the mother who bore you?

31 As long as the son of Jesse lives on this earth, neither you nor your kingdom will be established. Now send and bring him to me, for he must die!"

32 "Why should he be put to death? What has he done?" Jonathan asked his father.

33 But Saul hurled his spear at him to kill him. Then Jonathan knew that his father intended to kill David.

34 Jonathan got up from the table in fierce anger; on that second day of the month he did not eat, because he was grieved at his father's shameful treatment of David.
(1Sa 20:24-34 NIV)

Saul revealed his hatred for David. More than that, he attacked his son, both with his spear and with his tongue. What Saul said is ultimately more interesting than his actions. He told he is the *"... son of a perverse and rebellious woman!"* He is speaking of his wife, Ahinoam. This is curious because, in a couple of chapters we discover that David had escaped from Saul and relocated to Gath, together with his two wives, one of whom is also named Ahinoam. Some scholars have suggested that this is the same woman.

1 But David thought to himself, "One of these days I will be destroyed by the hand of Saul. The best thing I can do is to escape to the land of the Philistines. Then Saul will give up searching for me anywhere in Israel, and I will slip out of his hand."

2 So David and the six hundred men with him left and went over to Achish son of Maoch king of Gath.

3 David and his men settled in Gath with Achish. Each man had his family with him, and David had his two wives: Ahinoam of Jezreel and Abigail of Carmel, the widow of Nabal.
(1Sa 27:1-3 NIV)

Consider also the words of the prophet Nathan to David after he rebukes David with his parable of poor man's lamb:

7 Then Nathan said to David, "You are the man! This is what the LORD, the God of Israel, says: 'I anointed you king over Israel, and I delivered you from the hand of Saul.

8 I gave your master's house to you, and your master's wives into your arms. I gave you the house of Israel and Judah. And if all this had been too little, I would have given you even more.
(2Sa 12:7-8 NIV)

God delivered David's Master's wives into David's arms. David's master was Saul and Saul's wife was Ahinoam who Saul called a perverse and rebellious woman.

Anyway, for those of you who were concerned whether David got the message and want to see Jonathan's pledge of eternal cosmic kinship:

35 The next morning Jonathan, along with a young servant, went out to the field to meet David.

36 He said to his servant, "Run, find the arrows that I am about to shoot." As the servant ran, Jonathan shot the arrow beyond him.

37 When the servant came to the place where Jonathan had shot the arrow, Jonathan called out to the servant, "Isn't the arrow further beyond you?"

38 Jonathan called out to the servant, "Hurry! Go faster! Don't delay!" Jonathan's servant retrieved the arrow and came back to his master.

39 (Now the servant did not understand any of this. Only Jonathan and David knew what was going on.)

40 Then Jonathan gave his equipment to the servant who was with him. He said to him, "Go, take these things back to the city."

41 When the servant had left, David got up from beside the mound, knelt with his face to the ground, and bowed three times. Then they kissed each other and they both wept, especially David.

42 Jonathan said to David, "Go in peace, for the two of us have sworn together in the name of the LORD saying, 'The LORD will be between me and you and between my descendants and your descendants forever.'" Then David got up and left, while Jonathan went back to the city.
(1Sa 20:35-42 NET)

The next time we read of Jonathan, he has been killed together with his brothers and father in a battle against the Philistines. David said the following after learning of his death:

25 "How the mighty have fallen in battle! Jonathan lies slain on your heights.
26 I grieve for you, Jonathan my brother; you were very dear to me. Your love for me was wonderful, more wonderful than that of women.
(2Sa 1:25-26 NIV)

After reading David eulogy, I have images of David, Jonathan, and Ahinoam frolicking together in bed, but I'm sure that's only me. And so that is about it for Jonathan. He, along with Judah, Simeon, Levi, and Joseph all had some association with the archetype of the perverse woman or the prostitute, sacred or otherwise.

That leaves us with Melchi, Matthew, and Eliakim.

Melchi

Melchi means king and comes from the name Melchizedek who was a mysterious figure that appears in Genesis chapter fourteen.

18 Then Melchizedek king of Salem brought out bread and wine. He was priest of God Most High,
19 and he blessed Abram, saying, "Blessed be Abram by God Most High, Creator of heaven and earth.
20 And blessed be God Most High, who delivered your enemies into your hand." Then Abram gave him a tenth of everything.
(Gen 14:18-20 NIV)

He sort of comes out of nowhere, he is a king but also a priest. He brings out bread and wine, and Abram tithes his ten percent of everything he has. Strange, but then there is the psalm that David wrote about him:

Psalm 110:1 Of David. A psalm. The LORD says to my Lord: "Sit at my right hand until I make your enemies a footstool for your feet."

2 The LORD will extend your mighty scepter from Zion; you will rule in the midst of your enemies.

3 Your troops will be willing on your day of battle. Arrayed in holy majesty, from the womb of the dawn you will receive the dew of your youth.

4 The LORD has sworn and will not change his mind: "You are a priest forever, in the order of Melchizedek."

5 The Lord is at your right hand; he will crush kings on the day of his wrath.

6 He will judge the nations, heaping up the dead and crushing the rulers of the whole earth.

7 He will drink from a brook beside the way; therefore he will lift up his head.
(Psa 110:1-7 NIV)

A priest in the order of Melchizedek does a lot of king crushing apparently. The author of Matthew lets it be known that Melchizedek lurks somewhere behind the words Jesus employs to signal his intentions to his enemies without disturbing the faithful.

41 While the Pharisees were gathered together, Jesus asked them,

42 "What do you think about the Christ? Whose son is he?" "The son of David," they replied.

43 He said to them, "How is it then that David, speaking by the Spirit, calls him 'Lord'? For he says,

44 " 'The Lord said to my Lord: "Sit at my right hand until I put your enemies under your feet." '

45 If then David calls him 'Lord,' how can he be his son?"

46 No one could say a word in reply, and from that day on no one dared to ask him any more questions.
(Mat 22:41-46 NIV)

Finally, we come to Letter to the Hebrews where someone who almost certainly is not Paul lays out the significance of Melchizedek.

Hebrews 7:1 This Melchizedek was king of Salem and priest of God Most High. He met Abraham returning from the defeat of the kings and blessed him,

2 and Abraham gave him a tenth of everything. First, his name means "king of righteousness"; then also, "king of Salem" means "king of peace."

3 Without father or mother, without genealogy, without beginning of days or end of life, like the Son of God he remains a priest forever.

4 Just think how great he was: Even the patriarch Abraham gave him a tenth of the plunder!

5 Now the law requires the descendants of Levi who become priests to collect a tenth from the people--that is, their brothers-- even though their brothers are descended from Abraham.

6 This man, however, did not trace his descent from Levi, yet he collected a tenth from Abraham and blessed him who had the promises.

7 And without doubt the lesser person is blessed by the greater.

8 In the one case, the tenth is collected by men who die; but in the other case, by him who is declared to be living.

9 One might even say that Levi, who collects the tenth, paid the tenth through Abraham,

10 because when Melchizedek met Abraham, Levi was still in the body of his ancestor.

11 If perfection could have been attained through the Levitical priesthood (for on the basis of it the law was given to the people), why was there still need for another priest to come--one in the order of Melchizedek, not in the order of Aaron?

12 For when there is a change of the priesthood, there must also be a change of the law.

13 He of whom these things are said belonged to a different tribe, and no one from that tribe has ever served at the altar.

14 For it is clear that our Lord descended from Judah, and in regard to that tribe Moses said nothing about priests.

15 And what we have said is even more clear if another priest like Melchizedek appears,

16 one who has become a priest not on the basis of a regulation as to his ancestry but on the basis of the power of an indestructible life.

17 For it is declared: "You are a priest forever, in the order of Melchizedek."

(Heb 7:1-17 NIV)

The text from Hebrews tries to compare the priestly order of Melchizedek to the Levitical priesthood by claiming that the Levitical priesthood was based on tribe while that of Melchizedek was eternal. This is merely Platonism, making Melchizedek the higher idealized Form of the priesthood, while the Levites were a lower material manifestation of the Form.

A more relevant text concerning Melchizedek was found among the Dead Sea Scrolls. It is known as 11QMelch or the Melchizedek document (Vermes):

II... And concerning that which He said, In [this] year of Jubilee [each of you shall return to his property; and likewise, And this is the manner of release:] every creditor shall release that which he has lent [to his neighbor. He shall not exact it of his neighbor and his brother], for God's release [has been proclaimed]. [And it will be proclaimed at] the end of days concerning the captives as [He said, To proclaim liberty to the captives. Its interpretation is that He] will assign them to the Sons of Heaven and to the inheritance of Melchizedek; f[or He will cast] their [lot] amid the po[rtions of Melchize]dek, who will return them there and will proclaim to them liberty, forgiving them [the wrong-doings] of all their iniquities. And this thing will [occur] in the first week of the Jubilee that follows the nine Jubilees. And the Day of Atonement is the e[nd of the] tenth [Ju]bilee, when all the Sons of [Light] and the men of the lot of Mel[chi]zedek will be atoned for. [And] a statute concerns them [to prov]ide them with their rewards. For this is the moment of the Year of Grace for Melchizedek. [And h]e will, by his strength, judge the holy ones of God, executing judgement as it is written concerning him in the Songs of David, who said, ELOHIM has taken his place in the divine council; in the midst of the gods he holds judgement. And it was concerning him that he said, (Let the assembly of the peoples) return to the height above them; EL (god) will judge the peoples. As for that which he s[aid, How long will you] judge unjustly and show partiality to the wicked? Selah, its interpretation concerns Belial and the spirits of his lot [who] rebelled by turning away from the precepts of God to ... And Melchizedek will avenge the vengeance of the judgements of God... and he will drag [them from the hand of] Belial and from the hand of all the sp[irits of] his [lot].And all the 'gods [of Justice'] will come to his aid [to] attend to the de[struction] of Belial. And the height is ... all the sons of God...

this ... This is the day of [Peace/Salvation] concerning which [God]
spoke [through Isa]iah the prophet, who said, [How] beautiful upon
the mountains are the feet of the messenger who proclaims peace,
who brings good news, who proclaims salvation, who says to Zion:
Your ELOHIM [reigns]. Its interpretation; the mountains are the
prophets... and the messenger is the Anointed one of the spirit,
concerning whom Dan[iel] said, [Until an anointed one, a prince] ...
[And he who brings] good [news] , who proclaims [salvation]: it is
concerning him that it is written... [To comfort all who mourn, to
grant to those who mourn in Zion]. To comfort [those who mourn:
its interpretation], to make them understand all the ages of t[ime] ...
In truth ... will turn away from Belial... by the judgement[s] of God,
as it is written concerning him, [who says to Zion] ; your ELOHIM
reigns. Zion is ..., those who uphold the Covenant, who turn from
walking [in] the way of the people. And your ELOHIM is
[Melchizedek, who will save them from] the hand of Belial. As for
that which He said, Then you shall send abroad the trump[et in] all
the land ...

Essentially the text is a commentary of Leviticus 25. It mentions
that Melchizedek, rather than Michael, is leading God's angels in the
war against the rebellious angels. More importantly for our interests,
it describes Melchizedek as being Elohim, in other words, a divine
being, a member of Jehovah's council.

And yet, returning to the genealogy of Luke, the name Melchi
occurs twice. I am going to take this as referring to a bloodline that
stems from the priest-king Melchizedek, who was possibly the
archangel Michael and who appeared to Abram in Genesis within the
age of Taurus, which was ruled by the goddess Venus. On one side
we have the Hebrews maintaining the bloodline of the patriarchs,
beginning with Abraham, while at the same time we have the
matriarchs with their faithful wives and sacred prostitutes spinning
and preserving these other delicate lines of sacred genetics.

Matthew

The name Matthew in its various forms does not turn up until
the Hasmonean dynasty which is rather late, though I suspect that the
name indicates a specific profession rather than being the name of a

particular individual. We will return to the question of Matthew later in this volume, which leaves us with Eliakim.

Eliakim

The name Eliakim does not turn up in the Biblical record until Jehoiakim (c. 635–597 BC), the king of Judah, and from whom all later versions of the name are, according to Wikipedia, directly or indirectly derived. Jehoiakim was a poor king, but that is really beside the point since the name occurs in our list five generations after David which would be about three hundred years before Jehoiakim was born. Jehoiakim's birth name was Eliakim. Joachim is another form. However, regardless of the forms, it seems unlikely that the name refers to anyone significant historically.

The name is significant though. Not because of whom it originally belonged to, but of who eventually came to possess it.

The Genealogy of Mary

23 And Jesus himself began to be about thirty years of age, being (as was supposed) the son of Joseph, which was the son of Heli,
(Luk 3:23 KJV)

This beginning of the genealogy reads as though admitting that Joseph was not really the father of Jesus, but anyway here is the genealogy of Joseph going all the way back to Adam, even though it disagrees with the genealogy in Matthew for the same man. This being the case some have argued that this is actually the genealogy of Mary. This means that where it talks about Joseph being the son of Heli, actually it is Mary who is the daughter of Heli. Heli, some linguists contend, is a variant of Eli which is a shortened form of Eliakim. And Eliakim is a variant of Joachim.

As to why any of that matters, we must consider the text known as both the *Gospel of James* and the *Protevangelium of James*, an apocryphal text composed sometime in the mid to late 2nd century which purports to reveal more of the events that occurred both before the birth and during the infancy of Jesus. I should also point out before we begin that Ioacim is another rendering of Joachim.

The Protevangelium of James

I. 1 In the histories of the twelve tribes of Israel it is written that there was one Ioacim, exceeding rich: and he offered his gifts twofold, saying: That which is of my superfluity shall be for the whole people, and that which is for my forgiveness shall be for the Lord, for a propitiation unto me.

So this is our Ioacim, AKA Joachim, which is another form of Eliakim, of which Eli is a shorten form and which Heli is a variant of. Joachim means 'raised by Yahveh.' Eliakim means 'whom God will raise up.' He was wealthy and he wanted to make a considerable donation to Israel.

2 Now the great day of the Lord drew nigh and the children of Israel offered their gifts. And Reuben stood over against him saying: It is not lawful for thee to offer thy gifts first,-forasmuch as thou hast gotten no seed in Israel.

3 And Ioacim was sore grieved, and went unto the record of the twelve tribes of the people, saying: I will look upon the record of the twelve tribes of Israel, whether I only have not gotten seed in Israel. And he searched, and found concerning all the righteous that they had raised up seed in Israel. And he remembered the patriarch Abraham, how in the last days God gave him a son, even Isaac.

4 And Ioacim was sore grieved, and showed not himself to his wife, but betook himself into the wilderness, and pitched his tent there, and fasted forty days and forty nights, saying within himself: I will not go down either for meat or for drink until the Lord my God visit me, and my prayer shall be unto me meat and drink.

When Ioacim discovered that he could not give his gift because he had never fathered a child, he retreated to the wilderness and fasted for forty days and nights.

II Now his wife Anna lamented with two lamentations, and bewailed herself with two bewailings, saying: I will bewail my widowhood, and I will bewail my childlessness.

Scene change. Now we are with Ioacim's wife, Anna. She is upset both because she is childless and her husband has disappeared into the wilderness.

2 And the great day of the Lord drew nigh, and Judith her handmaid said unto her: How long humblest thou thy soul? The great day of the Lord hath come, and it is not lawful for thee to mourn: but take this headband, which the mistress of my work gave me, and it is not lawful for me to put it on, for as much as I am an handmaid, and it hath a mark of royalty. And Anna said: Get thee from me. Lo! I have done nothing (or I will not do so) and the Lord hath greatly humbled me: peradventure one gave it to thee in subtlety, and thou art come to make me partaker in thy sin. And Judith said: How shall I curse thee, seeing the Lord hath shut up thy womb, to give thee no fruit in Israel?

Then things get deep. It turns out that Anna has a handmaid named Judith. That name is quite significant, and we will return to that in a bit. For the moment we should focus on her actions. She tells Anna that she should not mourn anymore, that the day of the Lord has come. Then Judith pulls out a headband, or what reads like a diadem, a headband worn by royalty to denote their status. She tells the mistress of her work gave it to her, which likely means a priestess of the goddess. Anna does not respond well. She rebukes Judith. She accepts that her handmaid probably did not understand the significance of the headband, that an outside party was manipulating Judith into leading Anna into sin. Judith is like, what can God do to you beyond making you barren? Her work finished, she vanishes from the narrative.

3 And Anna was sore grieved [and mourned with a great mourning because she was reproached by all the tribes of Israel. And coming to herself she said: What shall I do? I will pray with weeping unto the Lord my God that he visit me]. And she put off her mourning garments and cleansed (or adorned) her head and put on her bridal garments: and about the ninth hour she went down into the garden to walk there. And she saw a laurel-tree and sat down underneath it and besought the Lord saying: O God of our fathers, bless me, and hearken unto my prayer, as thou didst bless the womb of Sarah, and gavest her a son, even Isaac.

Anna was like, fine, I will do what I swore never to do again. She puts on her bridal gown and the headband that marks her special status. We need to step back for a moment and consider who Anna is according to the genealogy in Luke.

So there were these eight pure bloodlines. Pure of course is a relative term in bloodlines especially when the dangers of inbreeding are taken into account and mitigated against. Also, my theory assumes that the followers of the goddess had a better understanding of the basics of the male and female contribution to the reproductive process than the followers of the patriarchal religion. Rather than keeping each line pure, it would be more a matter of keeping the lines separate from one another. Still, each line is sure to have stereotypical physiology and certain inbred deficiencies.

At the same time, the genealogy of Jesus shows the mixture of these ancient heroic bloodlines being applied sequentially like rare ingredients in a multi-generational alchemical operation. Anna was up to that point the culmination of this project and Ioacim, or if you prefer, Eliakim was her designated partner. Perhaps her importance to the followers of the goddess had been discovered by the followers of Jehovah, and she had been given a chance to live a normal life as long as she left the goddess cult behind her and served only Jehovah. She was then married to Eliakim, a very wealthy man, and all was well until he discovered that being without children would hold him back socially. And perhaps this had all unfolded according to the plans of the goddess, that Eliakim's sterility was not an accident. Instead it provided an opening for the divine to be seduced into contributing to the breeding project. If Eliakim is 'he who rises,' then his opposite is 'he who descends.'

III. 1 And looking up to the heaven she espied a nest of sparrows in the laurel-tree, and made a lamentation within herself, saying: Woe unto me, who begat me? And what womb brought me forth for I am become a curse before the children of Israel, and I am reproached, and they have mocked me forth out of the temple of the Lord? 2 Woe unto me, unto what am I likened? I am not likened unto the fowls of the heaven, for even the fowls of the heaven are fruitful before thee, O Lord. Woe unto me, unto what am I likened? I am not likened unto the beasts of the earth, for even the beasts of the earth are fruitful before thee, O Lord. Woe unto me, unto what am I likened? I am not likened unto these waters, for even these waters are fruitful before thee, O Lord. 3 Woe unto me, unto what am I likened? I am not likened unto this earth, for even this earth bringeth forth her fruits in due season and blesseth thee, O Lord.

Anna feels sorry for herself, praying before a nest of sparrows in a laurel-tree of the injustice of her infertility.

IV. 1 And behold an angel of the Lord appeared, saying unto her: Anna, Anna, the Lord hath hearkened unto thy prayer, and thou shalt conceive and bear, and thy seed shall be spoken of in the whole world. And Anna said: As the Lord my God liveth, if I bring forth either male or female, I will bring it for a gift unto the Lord my God, and it shall be ministering unto him all the days of its life.

Then an angel appeared and told her that she would have a child that would be famous throughout the whole world. Anna then promised that she would give the child as a gift to God and that it would minister to God for its entire life.

2 And behold there came two messengers saying unto her: Behold Ioacim thy husband cometh with his flocks: for an angel of the Lord came down unto him saying: Ioacim, Ioacim, the Lord God hath hearkened unto thy prayer. Get thee down hence, for behold thy wife Anna hath conceived. 3 And Ioacim sat him down and called his herdsmen saying: Bring me hither ten lambs without blemish and without spot, and they shall be for the Lord my God; and bring me twelve tender calves, and they shall be for the priests and for the assembly of the elders; and an hundred kids for the whole people.

Ioacim is thrilled by the news and prepares for a huge celebratory feast.

4 And behold Ioacim came with his flocks, and Anna stood at the gate and saw Ioacim coming, and ran and hung upon his neck, saying: Now know I that the Lord God hath greatly blessed me: for behold the widow is no more a widow, and she that was childless shall conceive. And Ioacim rested the first day in his house.

Good times for everybody.

V. 1 And on the morrow he offered his gifts, saying in himself: If the Lord God be reconciled unto me, the plate that is upon the forehead of the priest will make it manifest unto me. And Ioacim offered his gifts and looked earnestly upon the plate of the priest when he went up unto the altar of tile Lord, and he saw no sin in himself. And Ioacim said: Now know I that the Lord is become propitious unto me and hath forgiven all my sins. And he went down from the temple of the Lord justified, and went unto his house.

When he looked into the magic mirror strapped to the priest's forehead, no sign of sin. Good to go!

2 And her months were fulfilled, and in the ninth month Anna brought forth. And she said unto the midwife: what have I brought forth ? And she said: A female. And Anna said: My soul is magnified this day, and she laid herself down. And when the days were fulfilled, Anna purified herself and gave suck to the child and called her name Mary.

Anna went out and prayed to a sparrow's nest, and then an angel appeared and told her that she would conceive. Let us look at this as adults. Her husband played no role in her pregnancy other than increasing the pressure on her to conceive regardless of the costs and then stepping offstage. Anna wore her wedding dress and played the role of the sacred whore with the diadem of the goddess on her head. An angel appeared though I prefer to see him climbing down the tree. I suppose that one of the sparrows had gone and got the angel when the bird had spied Anna praying at the tree.

And so the angel fathered a daughter. But it would not have happened without the actions of Ioacim or Eliakim, 'whom God elevates.' Therefore I consider this name to indicate that the man in this position, through his own actions and sterility, essentially causes his mate to offer herself up to any interested angels. This name occurs twice in the Lukan genealogy, once in the beginning section being the second of the eight reoccurring names after a Matthew equivalent. This means that during the first half of the sequence an angel was evoked and contributed to the genetic makeup of the breeding project at the beginning of the series. Now, during the second half, an angel was summoned as the second to last contribution to the project. This turned out to be an unwise decision. This time the angel decided to stick around, maybe help out even more with the project. Who is next on the genealogy? Someone from the line of Joseph? The angel knew just how to find a qualifying candidate.

2 And when she was twelve years old, there was a council of the priests, saying: Behold Mary is become twelve years old in the temple of the Lord. What then shall we do with her? lest she pollute the sanctuary of the Lord. And they said unto the high priest: Thou standest over the altar of the Lord. Enter in and pray concerning her: And whatsoever the Lord shall reveal to thee, that let us do.

Notice how the section above provides a perfect segue way to the miracle of Darius' daughter and the bleeding woman.

3 And the high priest took the vestment with the twelve bells and went in unto the Holy of Holies and prayed concerning her. And lo, an angel of the Lord appeared saying unto him: Zacharias, Zacharias go forth and assemble them that are widowers of the people, and let them bring every man a rod, and to whomsoever the Lord shall show a sign, his wife shall she be. And the heralds went forth over all the country round about Judaea, and the trumpet of the Lord sounded, and all men ran thereto.

The angel appears to Zacharias in the Holy of Holies, and not for the last time.

IX. 1 And Joseph cast down his axe and ran to meet them, and when they were gathered together they went to the high priest and took their rods with them. And he took the rods of them all and went into the temple and prayed. And when he had finished the prayer he took the rods and went forth and gave them back to them: and there was no sign upon them. But Joseph received the last rod: and lo, a dove came forth of the rod and flew upon the bead of Joseph. And the priest said unto Joseph: Unto thee hath it fallen to take the virgin of the Lord and keep her for thyself. 2 And Joseph refused, saying: I have sons, and I am an old man, but she is a girl: lest I became a laughing-stock to the children of Israel. And the priest said unto Joseph: Hear the Lord thy God, and remember what things God did

82

unto Dathan and Abiram and Korah, how the earth clave and they were swallowed up because of their gainsaying. And now fear thou, Joseph, lest it be so in thine house. And Joseph was afraid, and took her to keep her for himself. And Joseph said unto Mary: Lo, I have received thee out of the temple of the Lord: and now do I leave thee in my house, and I go away to build my buildings and I will come again unto thee. The Lord shall watch over thee.

The angel delivered someone of the house of Joseph, but as he limited the pool to only widowers, this Joseph is already an old man. The priest threatens Joseph with the same fate as befell the three who rebelled against Moses if he refuses to take Mary as his wife. By finding someone from the house of Joseph, the genealogy is maintained. This seems to indicate that the last few entries on the genealogy ending with Jesus should be seen as predetermined. The sequence and number were set by the pattern.

Here are the sections of the genealogy running from Nathan to Salathiel and from Zorobabel to Jesus. As you will see that in both sections there are twenty-one generations.

Nathan	
Mattatha	Matthew
Menan	
Melea	
Eliakim	Eliakim
Jonam	John
Joseph	Joseph
Judah	Judah
Simeon	Simeon
Levi	Levi
Matthat	Matthew
Jorim	
Eliezer	
Jose	Joseph
Er	
Elmodam	
Cosam	
Addi	
Melchi	Melchi
Neri	
Salathiel	

Figure 10. Luke's genealogy from Nathan to Salathiel with variations identified.

Zorobabel	
Rhesa	
Joannan	John
Juda	Judah
Joseph	Joseph
Semei	Simeon
Mattathias	Matthew
Maath	
Nagge	
Esli	
Naum	
Amos	
Mattathias	Matthew
Joseph	Joseph
Jannai	
Melchi	Melchi
Levi	Levi
Matthat	Matthew
Heli	Eliakim
Joseph	Joseph
Jesus	

Figure 11. Luke's genealogy from Zorobabel to Jesus with variations identified.

Below we have the same two sections with all names removed except for the eight repeating names and their variants:

Mattatha	Matthew
Eliakim	Eliakim
Jonam	John
Joseph	Joseph
Judah	Judah
Simeon	Simeon
Levi	Levi
Matthat	Matthew
Jose	Joseph
Melchi	Melchi

Figure 12. Luke's genealogy from Nathan to Salathiel with all names removed except for the eight repeating names and their variants.

Joannan	John
Juda	Judah
Joseph	Joseph
Semei	Simeon
Mattathias	Matthew
Mattathias	Matthew
Joseph	Joseph
Melchi	Melchi
Levi	Levi
Matthat	Matthew
Heli	Eliakim
Joseph	Joseph

Figure 13. Luke's genealogy from Zorobabel to Jesus with all names removed except for the eight repeating names and their variants.

You will notice that the first section is two entries shorter than the second. This is because, while the first section has two repetitions of Matthew and Joseph, the second section has three repetitions of each name including variants. It is as though the breeders decided that while the first batch had double the quantity of Matthew and Joseph, the next batch needed even more. Also, note how Eliakim is the second in order in the first sequence and the second to last in the second. These indicators all point to a member of the Joseph bloodline being chosen to close out the series. But that is not what happened in this case.

At this point, I should probably address whether I believe either the text or what I am proposing the text actually means. My view is that I do not know whether a historical Jesus existed. My interest is not in determining whether the historical Jesus said or did this or that. My concern is what the texts say. My deeper interest is in those features of certain texts which remain hidden until brought to the surface which then change the meaning of the text in unexpected ways. Do I really think that followers of the goddess Venus had sacred prostitutes? Yes, that's clear from the historical record. Do I believe that these cults were able to maintain and cultivate ancient bloodlines stretching back thousands of years and that sometimes angels contributed to the manipulated gene-pools? I can only say that that is what I believe the texts are suggesting.

The authors who wrote the Synoptic Gospels hid information within the texts that would undermine the orthodox interpretation of the text by revealing an entire alternative system for understanding the world around and within them.

According to this alternative reading, Jesus was the product of a generation-long breeding program that got hijacked by an angel with an agenda during its penultimate step.

The Purple and Scarlet Threads

X. 1 Now there was a council of the priests, and they said: Let us make a veil for the temple of the Lord. And the priest said: Call unto me pure virgins of the tribe of David. And the officers departed and sought and found seven virgins. And the priests called to mind the child Mary, that she was of the tribe of avid and was undefiled before God: and the officers went and fetched her. And they brought them into the temple of the Lord, and the priest said: Cast me lots, which of you shah weave the gold and the undefiled (the white) and the fine linen and the silk and the hyacinthine, and the scarlet and the true purple. And the lot of the true purple and the scarlet fell unto Mary, and she took them and went unto her house. [And at that season Zacharias became dumb, and Samuel was in his stead until the time when Zacharias spake again.] But Mary took the scarlet and began to spin it.

The veil is made from seven sorts of thread. Mary is assigned the red and the purple. As we saw in the previous volume, red is the color of those associated with the goddess Venus. It concerns the nurturing and dispossessing of bloodlines through the women of the Biblical narrative. Purple is the color of royalty and perhaps represents Mary's connection to the bloodline of David through Nathan.

The angel's first vocal manifestation to Mary occurs after she begins to spin the red thread.

XL 1 And she took the pitcher and went forth to fill it with water: and lo a voice saying: Hail, thou that art highly favoured; the Lord is with thee: blessed art thou among women.

And she looked about her upon the right hand and upon the left, to see whence this voice should be: and being filled with trembling she went to her house and set down the pitcher, and took the purple and sat down upon her seat and drew out the thread.

Those listening to this tale must surely know that Mary needed only to look up to see the owner of the voice. Still, he does not appear to her until she begins to work with the purple thread.

2 And behold an angel of the Lord stood before her saying: Fear not, Mary, for thou hast found grace before the Lord of all things, and thou shalt conceive of his word. And she, when she heard it, questioned in herself, saying: Shall I verily conceive of the living God, and bring forth after the manner of all women? And the angel of the Lord said: Not so, Mary, for a power of the Lord shall overshadow thee: wherefore also that holy thing which shall be born of thee shall be called the Son of the Highest. And thou shalt call his name Jesus: for he shall save his people from their sins. And Mary said: Behold the handmaid of the Lord is before him: be it unto me according to thy word.

The angel impregnates Mary after setting all his sperm for male babies with angel magic, this seems to be a change from when Anna was made pregnant, and the gender of the child was undetermined. He is perhaps cooperating more closely with followers of the goddess and refining his abilities. He also assigned the child's name.

"Call the kid Jesus, or else you will mess up everything that I, I mean, everything that the Lord has got planned."

XII 1 And she made the purple and the scarlet and brought them unto the priest. And the priest blessed her and said: Mary, the Lord God hath magnified thy name, and thou shalt be blessed among all generations of the earth. 2 And Mary rejoiced and went away unto Elizabeth her kinswoman: and she knocked at the door. And Elizabeth when she heard it cast down the scarlet and ran to the door and opened it, and when she saw Mary she blessed her and said: Whence is this to me that the mother of my Lord should come unto me? for behold that which is in me leaped and blessed thee. And Mary forgat the mysteries which Gabriel the archangel had told her, and she looked up unto the heaven and said: Who am I, Lord, that all the generations of the earth do bless me? 8 And she abode three months with Elizabeth, and day by day her womb grew: and Mary was afraid and departed unto her house and hid herself from the children of Israel. Now she was sixteen years old when these mysteries came to pass.

Mary delivers the purple and red thread to the priests. Then she goes to visit her cousin Elizabeth. Elizabeth is also spinning thread, but of only one color, red. This likely represents the fact that she is part of the goddess's breeding project, but she does not carry royal blood herself.

5 In the time of Herod king of Judea there was a priest named Zechariah, who belonged to the priestly division of Abijah; his wife Elizabeth was also a descendant of Aaron.
6 Both of them were upright in the sight of God, observing all the Lord's commandments and regulations blamelessly.
7 But they had no children, because Elizabeth was barren; and they were both well along in years.
8 Once when Zechariah's division was on duty and he was serving as priest before God,
9 he was chosen by lot, according to the custom of the priesthood, to go into the temple of the Lord and burn incense.
10 And when the time for the burning of incense came, all the assembled worshipers were praying outside.

11 Then an angel of the Lord appeared to him, standing at the right side of the altar of incense.

12 When Zechariah saw him, he was startled and was gripped with fear.

(Luk 1:5-12 NIV)

Here from Luke, we see the same angel negotiating with Elizabeth's husband, Zechariah. But really Zechariah should not be too shocked. According to the *Protevangelium of James,* they had met here before, back when it had been time to find Mary a husband. Now, however, the angel needs to put the next stage of his plan into action, co-opting more pieces of the goddess' network of obedient followers to breed more semi-angelic progeny.

13 But the angel said to him: "Do not be afraid, Zechariah; your prayer has been heard. Your wife Elizabeth will bear you a son, and you are to give him the name John.

14 He will be a joy and delight to you, and many will rejoice because of his birth,

15 for he will be great in the sight of the Lord. He is never to take wine or other fermented drink, and he will be filled with the Holy Spirit even from birth.

16 Many of the people of Israel will he bring back to the Lord their God.

17 And he will go on before the Lord, in the spirit and power of Elijah, to turn the hearts of the fathers to their children and the disobedient to the wisdom of the righteous--to make ready a people prepared for the Lord."

18 Zechariah asked the angel, "How can I be sure of this? I am an old man and my wife is well along in years."

19 The angel answered, "I am Gabriel. I stand in the presence of God, and I have been sent to speak to you and to tell you this good news.

20 And now you will be silent and not able to speak until the day this happens, because you did not believe my words, which will come true at their proper time."

21 Meanwhile, the people were waiting for Zechariah and wondering why he stayed so long in the temple.

22 When he came out, he could not speak to them. They realized he had seen a vision in the temple, for he kept making signs to them but remained unable to speak.

23 When his time of service was completed, he returned home. (Luk 1:13-23 NIV)

Zechariah knows too much. Better that he be silenced until the birth.

24 After this his wife Elizabeth became pregnant and for five months remained in seclusion.

25 "The Lord has done this for me," she said. "In these days he has shown his favor and taken away my disgrace among the people."

26 In the sixth month, God sent the angel Gabriel to Nazareth, a town in Galilee,

27 to a virgin pledged to be married to a man named Joseph, a descendant of David. The virgin's name was Mary.

28 The angel went to her and said, "Greetings, you who are highly favored! The Lord is with you."

29 Mary was greatly troubled at his words and wondered what kind of greeting this might be.

30 But the angel said to her, "Do not be afraid, Mary, you have found favor with God.

31 You will be with child and give birth to a son, and you are to give him the name Jesus.

32 He will be great and will be called the Son of the Most High. The Lord God will give him the throne of his father David,

33 and he will reign over the house of Jacob forever; his kingdom will never end."

34 "How will this be," Mary asked the angel, "since I am a virgin?"

35 The angel answered, "The Holy Spirit will come upon you, and the power of the Most High will overshadow you. So the holy one to be born will be called the Son of God.

36 Even Elizabeth your relative is going to have a child in her old age, and she who was said to be barren is in her sixth month.

37 For nothing is impossible with God."

38 "I am the Lord's servant," Mary answered. "May it be to me as you have said." Then the angel left her.

(Luk 1:24-38 NIV)

Then amazingly Mary is made pregnant. This angel Gabriel has been making women pregnant for over a generation beginning with Mary's own mother. "Prepare to be overshadowed by the Most High. Yes, of course, you will still be a virgin (of the goddess). What? No, I didn't make a parenthetical comment."

39 At that time Mary got ready and hurried to a town in the hill country of Judea,
40 where she entered Zechariah's home and greeted Elizabeth.
41 When Elizabeth heard Mary's greeting, the baby leaped in her womb, and Elizabeth was filled with the Holy Spirit.
42 In a loud voice she exclaimed: "Blessed are you among women, and blessed is the child you will bear!
43 But why am I so favored, that the mother of my Lord should come to me?
44 As soon as the sound of your greeting reached my ears, the baby in my womb leaped for joy.
45 Blessed is she who has believed that what the Lord has said to her will be accomplished!"
(Luk 1:39-45 NIV)

Mary visits Elizabeth and the baby in Elizabeth's womb, John, leaps for joy because he recognizes Mary. Mary and John both have the angel's blood in their veins in equal measure, if we assume that the angel is the father of both. John and Mary are essentially half-siblings to one another. Their mothers were both believed to be infertile, Anna and Elizabeth. Then the angel Gabriel arrived and wombs were opened left and right.

56 Mary stayed with Elizabeth for about three months and then returned home.
57 When it was time for Elizabeth to have her baby, she gave birth to a son.
58 Her neighbors and relatives heard that the Lord had shown her great mercy, and they shared her joy.
59 On the eighth day they came to circumcise the child, and they were going to name him after his father Zechariah,
60 but his mother spoke up and said, "No! He is to be called John."

*61 They said to her, "There is no one among your relatives who
has that name."*

*62 Then they made signs to his father, to find out what he would
like to name the child.*

*63 He asked for a writing tablet, and to everyone's
astonishment he wrote, "His name is John."*

*64 Immediately his mouth was opened and his tongue was
loosed, and he began to speak, praising God.*
(Luk 1:56-64 NIV)

John is born. And like clockwork, six months later Jesus is born.

*21 On the eighth day, when it was time to circumcise him, he
was named Jesus, the name the angel had given him before he had
been conceived.*

*22 When the time of their purification according to the Law of
Moses had been completed, Joseph and Mary took him to Jerusalem
to present him to the Lord*

*23 (as it is written in the Law of the Lord, "Every firstborn male
is to be consecrated to the Lord"),*

*24 and to offer a sacrifice in keeping with what is said in the
Law of the Lord: "a pair of doves or two young pigeons."*

*25 Now there was a man in Jerusalem called Simeon, who was
righteous and devout. He was waiting for the consolation of Israel,
and the Holy Spirit was upon him.*

*26 It had been revealed to him by the Holy Spirit that he would
not die before he had seen the Lord's Christ.*

*27 Moved by the Spirit, he went into the temple courts. When
the parents brought in the child Jesus to do for him what the custom
of the Law required,*

28 Simeon took him in his arms and praised God, saying:

*29 "Sovereign Lord, as you have promised, you now dismiss
your servant in peace.*

30 For my eyes have seen your salvation,

31 which you have prepared in the sight of all people,

*32 a light for revelation to the Gentiles and for glory to your
people Israel."*

*33 The child's father and mother marveled at what was said
about him.*

*34 Then Simeon blessed them and said to Mary, his mother:
"This child is destined to cause the falling and rising of many in
Israel, and to be a sign that will be spoken against,*

*35 so that the thoughts of many hearts will be revealed. And a
sword will pierce your own soul too."*

*36 There was also a prophetess, Anna, the daughter of Phanuel,
of the tribe of Asher. She was very old; she had lived with her
husband seven years after her marriage,*

*37 and then was a widow until she was eighty-four. She never
left the temple but worshiped night and day, fasting and praying.*

*38 Coming up to them at that very moment, she gave thanks to
God and spoke about the child to all who were looking forward to
the redemption of Jerusalem.*

*39 When Joseph and Mary had done everything required by the
Law of the Lord, they returned to Galilee to their own town of
Nazareth.*

(Luk 2:21-39 NIV)

Jesus is eight days old, so Mom, Dad, and Baby Jesus had to
travel to Jerusalem. Basically, this three-unit family goes to
Jerusalem to pay taxes for having a baby which amounts to having a
priest sacrifice two pigeons. While waiting, they meet these two
characters. First is Simeon who was told that he would not die until
he saw 'the Lord's Christ' but now that he has seen baby Jesus he
knows he can die in peace.

Anna of the Tribe of Asher

Then there is Anna, a prophetess of the tribe of Asher. There are
very few prophetesses in the Bible. The word literally meant that she
was in contact with a divine being and was delivering messages on
its behalf. And what do we know about the tribe of Asher? Looking
back into the Old Testament we discover that:

*31 Nor did Asher drive out those living in Acco or Sidon or
Ahlab or Aczib or Helbah or Aphek or Rehob,*

*32 and because of this the people of Asher lived among the
Canaanite inhabitants of the land.*

(Jdg 1:31-32 NIV)

Above we see that Asher did not drive out the inhabitants of Sidon. In the next verses, we are told that Ashtoreth is the goddess of the Sidonians, the same tribe that the tribe of Asher failed to drive out above. More importantly, we learn that King Solomon himself worshiped Ashtoreth.

4 As Solomon grew old, his wives turned his heart after other gods, and his heart was not fully devoted to the LORD his God, as the heart of David his father had been.
5 He followed Ashtoreth the goddess of the Sidonians, and Molech the detestable god of the Ammonites.
(1Ki 11:4-5 NIV)

Jehovah was totally pissed.

11 So the LORD said to Solomon, "Since this is your attitude and you have not kept my covenant and my decrees, which I commanded you, I will most certainly tear the kingdom away from you and give it to one of your subordinates.
(1Ki 11:11 NIV)

33 I will do this because they have forsaken me and worshiped Ashtoreth the goddess of the Sidonians, Chemosh the god of the Moabites, and Molech the god of the Ammonites, and have not walked in my ways, nor done what is right in my eyes, nor kept my statutes and laws as David, Solomon's father, did.
(1Ki 11:33 NIV)

The focus for the worship of the goddess Ashtoreth was an Asherah pole as the following prohibition makes clear.

21 Do not set up any wooden Asherah pole beside the altar you build to the LORD your God,
22 and do not erect a sacred stone, for these the LORD your God hates.
(Deu 16:21-22 NIV)

In addition, the tribe Asher, the goddess Ashtoreth, and the Asherah poles all share the root 'ashar' which means to be straight,

straight used in the broadest sense, especially to be level, right, and happy. Beyond this linguistic evidence, we have the verses above which show a clear connection between the tribe of Asher and the worship of the goddess Ashtoreth, whose other forms include Astarte, Ishtar, and Isis.

Asher was also one of the twelve tribes mentioned in the Blessing of Jacob:

20 Out of Asher his bread shall be fat, and he shall yield royal dainties.
(Gen 49:20 KJV)

That is interesting as Asher provides a pretty clear connection between the tribe associated with baking bread and with the goddess Venus.

Anna, Daughter of Phanuel

Back to Anna, the prophetess of the tribe of Asher, who was said to be waiting for the redeemer of Jerusalem, though it seems more likely that she was an agent of the goddess assigned to get eyes on baby Jesus and confirm his birth. Perhaps the followers of the goddess were waiting for a savior of their own. One interesting aspect of Anna's introduction is that she is described as the daughter of Phanuel. Phanuel was the name of one of the four archangels who stand before God in the Book of Enoch (Charles, 1917) along with Michael, Raphael, and Gabriel. And Gabriel, if you need reminding, is the name of the angel that has been appearing to people and making women pregnant.

1. And it came to pass after this that my spirit was translated
And it ascended into the heavens:
And I saw the holy sons of God.

They were stepping on flames of fire:
Their garments were white [and their raiment],
And their faces shone like snow.

2. And I saw two streams of fire,
And the light of that fire shone like hyacinth,

And I fell on my face before the Lord of Spirits.

*3. And the angel Michael [one of the archangels] seized me by
my right hand,*
And lifted me up and led me forth into all the secrets,
And he showed me all the secrets of righteousness.

4. And he showed me all the secrets of the ends of the heaven,
And all the chambers of all the stars, and all the luminaries,
Whence they proceed before the face of the holy ones.

5. And he translated my spirit into the heaven of heavens,
And I saw there as it were a structure built of crystals,
And between those crystals tongues of living fire.

6. And my spirit saw the girdle which girt that house of fire,
And on its four sides were streams full of living fire,
And they girt that house.p. 94

7. And round about were Seraphin, Cherubic, and Ophannin:
And these are they who sleep not
And guard the throne of His glory.

8. And I saw angels who could not be counted,
A thousand thousands, and ten thousand times ten thousand,
Encircling that house.

And Michael, and Raphael, and Gabriel, and Phanuel,
And the holy angels who are above the heavens,
Go in and out of that house.
(The Book of Enoch Chapter 71 v.1-8)

There is a remote possibility that this Anna actually is the same
woman who married Eliakim and mothered Mary. If you recall,
Mary's mother's name was also Anna. If this is meant to be the same
woman, then the text suggests that she was married to her husband
Ioacim for only seven years before he died. From this, we can
determine that she had been married for no more than four years
before she gave birth to Mary because Ioacim is present in the
Protevangelium of James right up to Mary's third year after which

97

he disappears from the narrative. According to the *Protevangelium of James,* Mary was sixteen when she got pregnant, so if Anna gave birth to her sixteen years before the present and she is eighty-four now, that means she had Mary when Anna was sixty-eight, which would also suggest that her husband Ioacim died when she was probably around seventy-two. This seems unlikely because the text never mentioned that Anna was especially old, however, if her father was the archangel Phanuel and if we assume that angels possessed immortality or at least great longevity, then Anna may not have appeared her actual chronological age.

The more likely possibility is that the term 'daughter of Phanuel' is meant to be understood as Anna being a descendant of Phanuel from some time generations ago. Perhaps Phanuel was the angel that was brought into the genealogy by the first Eliakem around thirty-five generations ago. If that were the case, then some thirty-five generations ago, when an Eliakim brought down an angel to inject the divine into a generations-long breeding project being conducted by the followers of the goddess, it was Phanuel that was seduced or perhaps more correctly evoked and bound, then used and released. From that time forward the women born into this particular breeding line would have been known as the daughters of Phanuel. Assuming that is the case, then Anna was the last daughter of Phanuel and her daughter, Mary, was the first daughter of Gabriel. And Mary's son was the long-awaited culmination of a breeding project spanning ages of time.

The Hidden Mythos

40 And the child grew and became strong; he was filled with wisdom, and the grace of God was upon him.

41 Every year his parents went to Jerusalem for the Feast of the Passover.

42 When he was twelve years old, they went up to the Feast, according to the custom.

43 After the Feast was over, while his parents were returning home, the boy Jesus stayed behind in Jerusalem, but they were unaware of it.

44 Thinking he was in their company, they traveled on for a day. Then they began looking for him among their relatives and friends.

45 When they did not find him, they went back to Jerusalem to look for him.

46 After three days they found him in the temple courts, sitting among the teachers, listening to them and asking them questions.

47 Everyone who heard him was amazed at his understanding and his answers.

48 When his parents saw him, they were astonished. His mother said to him, "Son, why have you treated us like this? Your father and I have been anxiously searching for you."

49 "Why were you searching for me?" he asked. "Didn't you know I had to be in my Father's house?"

50 But they did not understand what he was saying to them.

51 Then he went down to Nazareth with them and was obedient to them. But his mother treasured all these things in her heart.

(Luk 2:40-51 NIV)

Here we have the story of the twelve-year-old Jesus going missing while on a trip with his parents to Jerusalem. His parents searched everywhere for him until they found him in the temple courts where he was asking questions of the teachers and amazing them with his understanding. His mother asks him why he treated them in such a manner. He asks why they are searching for his when he would obviously be at his father's house. His parents did not understand, but Mary kept these things in her heart, where she could consider them later.

Jesus was at the Jerusalem temple. He told his parents that he was at his father's house. His parents do not understand the significance of his answer, but we are meant to understand that Jesus was referring to God as his father. Since he was at the temple, he was at God's house, which is to say, his father's house. We, the readers of the Gospels, understand what Jesus means even as his parents do not. But Mary, she could at least look back and gain an understanding of what her son said. What if we were to do the same?

What if Jesus does not mean that as he was the Son of God, that his being at the temple should have been obvious because the temple was God's, which is to say, his Father's house? What if he actually meant that they should have gone looking for him at his biological father's house? That would mean that the temple somehow belonged both to God and this man, or rather this angel posing as a man.

The Human Father of Jesus

The idea that Jesus had a human father is not a new one. In the second century, the Greek philosopher Celsus wrote that Jesus was fathered by a Roman soldier named Pantera. Origen wrote attacking this view, this is the only record we have that Celsus made such a claim.

Let us return, however, to the words put into the mouth of the Jew, where "the mother of Jesus" is described as having been "turned out by the carpenter who was betrothed to her, as she had been convicted of adultery and had a child by a certain soldier named Panthera."

The idea that Jesus was fathered by a man named Pantera is found in the Talmud, but the origin of the story is considered to date from at best the four century, and these stories are considered anti-Christian fictions written to parody the new religion. Pantera, meaning panther, was a common name among Roman soldiers. Marcus J. Borg and John Dominic Crossan have suggested that the word was chosen due to its similarity to the Greek word for virgin, 'Parthenos' to make a not so subtle play on words.

I am not suggesting that Jesus had a Roman soldier named Pantera for a father. Rather, my theory is that the Synoptic Gospels were written in such a manner that allows one to find various clues which all point to one individual being identified as the biological father of Jesus, and that entity is also the angel identified as Gabriel in Luke and the apocryphal sources. This identification will force us to reevaluate all of the relationships among the well-known characters of the Jesus story transforming it into an almost unrecognizable diorama of betrayal and tragedy that will forever change our understanding of this cultural mythos.

So, where to begin? The Gospel of Philip (Isenberg, 1988) encourages us with:

And the Lord would not have said: "My Father who is in Heaven," unless he had had another father, but he would have said simply "My father."
(GoPh 18)

The Three Marys

In much the same vein the text provides a clue that we are on the same page with the following little tidbit:

There were three who always walked with the Lord: Mary, his mother, and her sister, and Magdalene, the one who was called his companion. His sister and his mother and his companion were each a Mary.
(GoPh 36)

We know about Mary his mother, and Mary Magdalene, his companion, but Mary his sister?

The Synoptic Gospels do not give us much to go on.

1 Jesus left there and went to his hometown, accompanied by his disciples.
2 When the Sabbath came, he began to teach in the synagogue, and many who heard him were amazed. "Where did this man get these things?" they asked. "What's this wisdom that has been given him, that he even does miracles!
3 Isn't this the carpenter? Isn't this Mary's son and the brother of James, Joseph, Judas and Simon? Aren't his sisters here with us?" And they took offense at him.

4 Jesus said to them, "Only in his hometown, among his relatives and in his own house is a prophet without honor."

5 He could not do any miracles there, except lay his hands on a few sick people and heal them.

6 And he was amazed at their lack of faith. Then Jesus went around teaching from village to village.

(Mar 6:1-6 NIV)

Mark mentions four brothers and an uncertain plurality of sisters. Matthew repeats the information with an even greater economy of words.

54 Coming to his hometown, he began teaching the people in their synagogue, and they were amazed. "Where did this man get this wisdom and these miraculous powers?" they asked.

55 "Isn't this the carpenter's son? Isn't his mother's name Mary, and aren't his brothers James, Joseph, Simon and Judas?

56 Aren't all his sisters with us? Where then did this man get all these things?"

57 And they took offense at him. But Jesus said to them, "Only in his hometown and in his own house is a prophet without honor."

58 And he did not do many miracles there because of their lack of faith.

(Mat 13:54-58 NIV)

While we do have information that Jesus had some number of sisters, we do not know their names. Perhaps one of them was named Mary after their mother. It wouldn't be unheard of. Still, the verse from the Gospel of Philip seems to be getting at something more than significant than Jesus had an unknown sister named Mary. The way the text is structured, Mary the sister of Jesus should be just as significant as Mary his mother and Mary Magdalene, yet how could that be if no one had ever learned her name?

To solve this paradox we need only to return to the genealogical drama as played out in the *Protevangelium of James*. Gabriel impregnates Anna, Mary's mother, thereby fathering Mary. Gabriel then impregnates Mary and fathers Jesus. Mary is the mother of Jesus, but she is also his half-sister as they share the same father. But their relationship goes well beyond this. Consider the scene from the

Synoptic Gospels when Jesus refuses to meet with his family by announcing that those who follow God's word are his family.

> *19 Now Jesus' mother and brothers came to see him, but they were not able to get near him because of the crowd.*
> *20 Someone told him, "Your mother and brothers are standing outside, wanting to see you."*
> *21 He replied, "My mother and brothers are those who hear God's word and put it into practice."*
> *(Luk 8:19-21 NIV)*

The section above from Luke is the most context-free out of the various versions. When read in situ, the section seems to have been dropped between two totally unrelated sections.

The section from Matthew, however, does seem to be embedded next to a relevant section of text:

> *38 Then some of the Pharisees and teachers of the law said to him, "Teacher, we want to see a miraculous sign from you."*
> *39 He answered, "A wicked and adulterous generation asks for a miraculous sign! But none will be given it except the sign of the prophet Jonah.*
> *40 For as Jonah was three days and three nights in the belly of a huge fish, so the Son of Man will be three days and three nights in the heart of the earth.*
> *41 The men of Nineveh will stand up at the judgment with this generation and condemn it; for they repented at the preaching of Jonah, and now one greater than Jonah is here.*
> *42 The Queen of the South will rise at the judgment with this generation and condemn it; for she came from the ends of the earth to listen to Solomon's wisdom, and now one greater than Solomon is here.*
> *43 "When an evil spirit comes out of a man, it goes through arid places seeking rest and does not find it.*
> *44 Then it says, 'I will return to the house I left.' When it arrives, it finds the house unoccupied, swept clean and put in order.*
> *45 Then it goes and takes with it seven other spirits more wicked than itself, and they go in and live there. And the final condition of that man is worse than the first. That is how it will be with this wicked generation."*

46 While Jesus was still talking to the crowd, his mother and brothers stood outside, wanting to speak to him.

47 Someone told him, "Your mother and brothers are standing outside, wanting to speak to you."

48 He replied to him, "Who is my mother, and who are my brothers?"

49 Pointing to his disciples, he said, "Here are my mother and my brothers.

50 For whoever does the will of my Father in heaven is my brother and sister and mother."

(Mat 12:38-50 NIV)

First, the Pharisees ask for a sign, and then Jesus gives two examples of people who accepted the prophecy and wisdom of people much less exalted than one who is there now. Then he provides a third example which does not seem to have anything to do with the section concerning Jonah and Solomon. Instead, it has to do with an evil spirit who leaves a person, where the translation has the word 'man,' the original Greek word was 'anthropos,' which means human being of either gender. The evil spirit goes looking for peace but cannot find it, so it returns to the person it had left. When it returns, it finds the house empty, clean, and in order. The evil spirit then goes and finds seven spirits even eviler than itself, and they all move into that person. Then Jesus says that that is what is going to happen to the present generation which does not make much sense. Finally, he is told that his mother and brothers are outside, to which he replies that those who do the will of the father are his family.

Finally, we come to the earliest version, which is found in Mark. This first little section from early in the chapter helps create context:

6 Then the Pharisees went out and began to plot with the Herodians how they might kill Jesus.

7 Jesus withdrew with his disciples to the lake, and a large crowd from Galilee followed.

(Mar 3:6-7 NIV)

Jesus had pushed the Pharisees to the point that they began to plot his murder with the help of the Herodians. Still, Jesus continued to grow in popularity.

20 Then Jesus entered a house, and again a crowd gathered, so that he and his disciples were not even able to eat.

21 When his family heard about this, they went to take charge of him, for they said, "He is out of his mind."

22 And the teachers of the law who came down from Jerusalem said, "He is possessed by Beelzebub! By the prince of demons he is driving out demons."

23 So Jesus called them and spoke to them in parables: "How can Satan drive out Satan?

24 If a kingdom is divided against itself, that kingdom cannot stand.

25 If a house is divided against itself, that house cannot stand.

26 And if Satan opposes himself and is divided, he cannot stand; his end has come.

27 In fact, no one can enter a strong man's house and carry off his possessions unless he first ties up the strong man. Then he can rob his house.

28 I tell you the truth, all the sins and blasphemies of men will be forgiven them.

29 But whoever blasphemes against the Holy Spirit will never be forgiven; he is guilty of an eternal sin."

30 He said this because they were saying, "He has an evil spirit."

31 Then Jesus' mother and brothers arrived. Standing outside, they sent someone in to call him.

32 A crowd was sitting around him, and they told him, "Your mother and brothers are outside looking for you."

33 "Who are my mother and my brothers?" he asked.

34 Then he looked at those seated in a circle around him and said, "Here are my mother and my brothers!

35 Whoever does God's will is my brother and sister and mother."

(Mar 3:20-35 NIV)

In the section above, Mark lays the situation out clearly. Jesus was traveling with a growing crowd. His family heard about it and went to get him, claiming that "He is out of his mind." This idea is then amplified by some lawyers from Jerusalem who accused him of being possessed by Beelzebub and that the prince of demons is helping Jesus to drive out demons. Jesus then turns this argument on its head and asks how Satan can drive out Satan. He says that a kingdom divided against itself cannot stand and that a house divided against itself also cannot stand. Then comes reports that his mother and brothers are looking for him. He looks at those seated in a circle around him and says, "Here are my mother and my brothers! Whoever does God's will is my brother and sister and mother."

Do you notice the incongruity? On the one hand, we have the family of Jesus claiming that he is mad and on the other hand we have Jesus stating that a house divided against itself cannot stand. This is usually associated with the bit about Beelzebub driving out demons, but actually, the initial event is the attack on Jesus by his family.

Look again at the chain of events. First, the Pharisees start plotting with the Herodians on how to kill Jesus. Then the family of Jesus appears and claims that he has lost his mind and that they are there to take care of him. To this Jesus brings up the fact that a house divided will fall. Then he is told that his mother and brothers are outside looking for him, to which he replies that those sitting around him are in fact his mother and brothers. This can be understood in two ways.

The first way is the traditional understanding that yes, his biological family has come for him, but these people around him are his spiritual family. The alternative explanation is that the family outside is fake. It is all part of a trick devised by the Pharisees and the Herodians to trick Jesus into letting a group of disguised soldiers get close enough to Jesus to capture him, all under the guise of retrieving their crazy relative. The reason this ploy fails is that the mother and brothers of Jesus have been part of his inner circle all along.

Seven Unclean Spirits

Let us go back to the version from Matthew with the parable of the seven unclean spirits which has a rather unusual parallel in Luke:

24 "When an evil spirit comes out of a man, it goes through arid places seeking rest and does not find it. Then it says, 'I will return to the house I left.'
25 When it arrives, it finds the house swept clean and put in order.

26 Then it goes and takes seven other spirits more wicked than itself, and they go in and live there. And the final condition of that man is worse than the first."

27 As Jesus was saying these things, a woman in the crowd called out, "Blessed is the mother who gave you birth and nursed you."

28 He replied, "Blessed rather are those who hear the word of God and obey it."

(Luk 11:24-28 NIV)

The parable of evil spirit returning with seven even more wicked spirits concludes with a woman blessing Jesus' mother, which he then turns around and says that those who hear and follow the word of God are blessed. Why I find this especially significant is the manner in which it links the person with the evil spirits to the mother of Jesus and then furthermore links it all back to Jesus claiming that his real family is composed of those who listen to and obey God.

The text would seem to suggest that the person who had been liberated from seven evil spirits was actually the mother of Jesus. But we have evidence that it was Mary Magdalene who was cured of demon possession by seven demons, though there is still one unaccounted for as the text implies the presence of eight.

9 When Jesus rose early on the first day of the week, he appeared first to Mary Magdalene, out of whom he had driven seven demons.

(Mar 16:9 NIV)

1 After this, Jesus traveled about from one town and village to another, proclaiming the good news of the kingdom of God. The Twelve were with him,

2 and also some women who had been cured of evil spirits and diseases: Mary (called Magdalene) from whom seven demons had come out;

3 Joanna the wife of Cuza, the manager of Herod's household; Susanna; and many others. These women were helping to support them out of their own means.

(Luk 8:1-3 NIV)

Or, as the Gospel of Thomas subtly puts it:

Jesus said: "Whoever knows father and mother will be called the son of a whore.
(GoT 105)

A reminder of what the Gospel of Philip adds to the mix:

There were three who always walked with the Lord: Mary, his mother, and her sister, and Magdalene, the one who was called his companion. His sister and his mother and his companion were each a Mary.
(GoPh 36)

Mary: Sister, Mother, and Sacred Whore

The texts point to there being a single Mary: Sister, mother, and sacred whore. Let us suppose that the brothers of Jesus are boys of the pure bloodlines. However, one of the names of the brothers of Jesus is not among the eight names associated with the pure bloodlines, James, Jacob in Hebrew. It seems that Gabriel may have fathered another son with Mary after Jesus.

Still, Gabriel would want to run as many of the old pure bloodlines through Mary as possible. This is to spread her semi-divine nature across the maximum number of bloodlines. So a Joseph was bred, and a Judah, and a Simon. And several sisters. In each case, a father from a different bloodline has been brought forward to mate with Mary and produce a child. Or at least that is the theory that I have concocted.

This, combined with the seven demons being expelled from Mary, leads me to think that the parable of the woman with seven husbands is connected to her as well:

18 Then the Sadducees, who say there is no resurrection, came to him with a question.
19 "Teacher," they said, "Moses wrote for us that if a man's brother dies and leaves a wife but no children, the man must marry the widow and have children for his brother.
20 Now there were seven brothers. The first one married and died without leaving any children.

21 The second one married the widow, but he also died, leaving no child. It was the same with the third.

22 In fact, none of the seven left any children. Last of all, the woman died too.

23 At the resurrection whose wife will she be, since the seven were married to her?"

24 Jesus replied, "Are you not in error because you do not know the Scriptures or the power of God?

25 When the dead rise, they will neither marry nor be given in marriage; they will be like the angels in heaven.

26 Now about the dead rising--have you not read in the book of Moses, in the account of the bush, how God said to him, 'I am the God of Abraham, the God of Isaac, and the God of Jacob'?

27 He is not the God of the dead, but of the living. You are badly mistaken!"

(Mar 12:18-27 NIV)

This is repeated in both Matthew and Luke with few changes. I think that When Jesus asserts at the end that God is not the God of the dead, but of the living, that the parable should be understood to be about living people. The husbands do not die, and they actually do father children. But when one husband leaves another comes until the next child is born. And so on and so forth and that this is what this story was indicating life for Mary was like.

9 When Jesus rose early on the first day of the week, he appeared first to Mary Magdalene, out of whom he had driven seven demons.

(Mar 16:9 NIV)

My feeling is that the text indicates that Jesus had saved Mary from this role as the breeder for Gabriel. I suppose if this adventure did occur that it took place when Jesus was in his teens. He saw how his mother was being used to breed these various children from a steady parade of fathers. Together Mary and Jesus fled, deep with the territory of the goddess, beyond the reaches of the angel Gabriel. There they found refuge and Jesus received his schooling in the hidden secrets of the ages as well as what his father had planned for him and his brother. Or so I imagine.

Astrologically each age is ruled by a planet. The age of Pisces was ruled by Jupiter. Jupiter also rules the sign of Sagittarius, whose symbol is the archer. The animal associated with the archer is the bird, given that arrows fly. This is all outlined in volume three. Let us just take as a given that Jupiter is associated with fish and birds.

John with his baptism was the fish, while Jesus was to be the bird, a divine being with the power to fulfill his will. Jesus is represented by two colors of thread, one red and the other purple, while John is associated with a single red thread. Red indicates that both men came from manipulated bloodlines, while the purple is the color of royalty. Birds symbolize royalty while fish represent the poor dreaming masses.

John stayed with his father Gabriel and the rest of his brothers, building his group, while Jesus escaped with Mary back to the source and learned the mysteries of the goddess. This knowledge came with a hefty price, for no man was permitted to know of the inner secrets of the goddess. I base this on the story of Callo by Diodorus Siculus, which I presented in the first chapter.

Mary was a priestess of the goddess, and she loved Jesus, her son and brother, in the way of the ancient Egyptians, and she had no intention of allowing Jesus to mirror Osiris in that regard. An exception was made in Jesus' case, but it was less an exception and more a postponement. Jesus had to pay the price, or perhaps, see that it was paid by a satisfactory surrogate before he could actively fulfill his part in his father's plan or else Jesus would incur the wrath of the goddess. At least that is how I see things developing based on events to come within the narrative.

For now, let us check in with John:

1 The beginning of the gospel about Jesus Christ, the Son of God.

2 It is written in Isaiah the prophet: "I will send my messenger ahead of you, who will prepare your way"--

3 "a voice of one calling in the desert, 'Prepare the way for the Lord, make straight paths for him.' "

4 And so John came, baptizing in the desert region and preaching a baptism of repentance for the forgiveness of sins.

5 The whole Judean countryside and all the people of Jerusalem went out to him. Confessing their sins, they were baptized by him in the Jordan River.

6 John wore clothing made of camel's hair, with a leather belt around his waist, and he ate locusts and wild honey.

7 And this was his message: "After me will come one more powerful than I, the thongs of whose sandals I am not worthy to stoop down and untie.

8 I baptize you with water, but he will baptize you with the Holy Spirit."

(Mar 1:1-8 NIV)

Mark keeps it simple. John is out there, preparing for Jesus to show up. Notice the bit about John not being worthy to untie Jesus' sandals. You will recall that the Bible frequently uses 'feet' as a euphemism for 'genitals.' This would seem to be a reference to the sacrifice Jesus is expected to undergo. At the same time, it reads like an insult that John apparently heard time and again in reference to his younger brother from another mother, meaning that essentially John was not worthy to ungird Jesus' loins. Then John says that bit about John's baptism being with water while Jesus' will be with the Holy Spirit.

1 In those days John the Baptist came, preaching in the Desert of Judea

2 and saying, "Repent, for the Kingdom of Heaven is near."

3 This is he who was spoken of through the prophet Isaiah: "A voice of one calling in the desert, 'Prepare the way for the Lord, make straight paths for him.' "

4 John's clothes were made of camel's hair, and he had a leather belt around his waist. His food was locusts and wild honey.

5 People went out to him from Jerusalem and all Judea and the whole region of the Jordan.

6 Confessing their sins, they were baptized by him in the Jordan River.

7 But when he saw many of the Pharisees and Sadducees coming to where he was baptizing, he said to them: "You brood of vipers! Who warned you to flee from the coming wrath?

8 Produce fruit in keeping with repentance.

9 And do not think you can say to yourselves, 'We have Abraham as our father.' I tell you that out of these stones God can raise up children for Abraham.

10 The ax is already at the root of the trees, and every tree that does not produce good fruit will be cut down and thrown into the fire.
11 "I baptize you with water for repentance. But after me will come one who is more powerful than I, whose sandals I am not fit to carry. He will baptize you with the Holy Spirit and with fire.
12 His winnowing fork is in his hand, and he will clear his threshing floor, gathering his wheat into the barn and burning up the chaff with unquenchable fire."
(Mat 3:1-12 NIV)

Matthew likes to lay on the hellfire. Notice how Mark only had Jesus baptizing with Holy Spirit, but Matthew adds fire to the mix as well as wheat. If we assume that Jesus baptizing with Holy Spirit is referring to using ergot-infected grain, then the fire might be a reference to the feeling of intense burning pain that sometimes results. Another way to look at it astrologically is that Pisces is a water sign and Sagittarius is a fire sign. And birds do have more to do with grain than fish. So everything John says seems to point towards John saying that he is just a fish, but in a little while, a bird is going to come and burn this place to the ground.

1 In the fifteenth year of the reign of Tiberius Caesar--when Pontius Pilate was governor of Judea, Herod tetrarch of Galilee, his brother Philip tetrarch of Iturea and Traconitis, and Lysanias tetrarch of Abilene--
2 during the high priesthood of Annas and Caiaphas, the word of God came to John son of Zechariah in the desert.
3 He went into all the country around the Jordan, preaching a baptism of repentance for the forgiveness of sins.
4 As is written in the book of the words of Isaiah the prophet: "A voice of one calling in the desert, 'Prepare the way for the Lord, make straight paths for him.
5 Every valley shall be filled in, every mountain and hill made low. The crooked roads shall become straight, the rough ways smooth.
6 And all mankind will see God's salvation.' "
7 John said to the crowds coming out to be baptized by him, "You brood of vipers! Who warned you to flee from the coming wrath?

8 Produce fruit in keeping with repentance. And do not begin to say to yourselves, 'We have Abraham as our father.' For I tell you that out of these stones God can raise up children for Abraham.

9 The ax is already at the root of the trees, and every tree that does not produce good fruit will be cut down and thrown into the fire."

10 "What should we do then?" the crowd asked.

11 John answered, "The man with two tunics should share with him who has none, and the one who has food should do the same."

12 Tax collectors also came to be baptized. "Teacher," they asked, "what should we do?"

13 "Don't collect any more than you are required to," he told them.

14 Then some soldiers asked him, "And what should we do?" He replied, "Don't extort money and don't accuse people falsely--be content with your pay."

15 The people were waiting expectantly and were all wondering in their hearts if John might possibly be the Christ.

16 John answered them all, "I baptize you with water. But one more powerful than I will come, the thongs of whose sandals I am not worthy to untie. He will baptize you with the Holy Spirit and with fire.

17 His winnowing fork is in his hand to clear his threshing floor and to gather the wheat into his barn, but he will burn up the chaff with unquenchable fire."

18 And with many other words John exhorted the people and preached the good news to them.

19 But when John rebuked Herod the tetrarch because of Herodias, his brother's wife, and all the other evil things he had done,

20 Herod added this to them all: He locked John up in prison. (Luk 3:1-20 NIV)

Luke follows Matthew while adding a few more details and some historical backstory. Then finally along comes Jesus.

9 At that time Jesus came from Nazareth in Galilee and was baptized by John in the Jordan.

10 As Jesus was coming up out of the water, he saw heaven being torn open and the Spirit descending on him like a dove.

11 And a voice came from heaven: "You are my Son, whom I love; with you I am well pleased."
(Mar 1:9-11 NIV)

Mark gives us the bare bones version of Jesus being baptized, though the heavens being torn open is a nice touch.

21 When all the people were being baptized, Jesus was baptized too. And as he was praying, heaven was opened
22 and the Holy Spirit descended on him in bodily form like a dove. And a voice came from heaven: "You are my Son, whom I love; with you I am well pleased."
(Luk 3:21-22 NIV)

Luke's version above is the most generic of the three.

13 Then Jesus came from Galilee to the Jordan to be baptized by John.
14 But John tried to deter him, saying, "I need to be baptized by you, and do you come to me?"
15 Jesus replied, "Let it be so now; it is proper for us to do this to fulfill all righteousness." Then John consented.
16 As soon as Jesus was baptized, he went up out of the water. At that moment heaven was opened, and he saw the Spirit of God descending like a dove and lighting on him.
17 And a voice from heaven said, "This is my Son, whom I love; with him I am well pleased."
(Mat 3:13-17 NIV)

Matthew adds the bit about Jesus being supposed to baptize John. What seems to be happening here is that according to the plan, Jesus was supposed to baptize John and not be baptized by John, which makes sense if Jesus is representative of a bird. His baptism of John would confirm John's identity as a fish. Jesus refusing to baptize him signals to John that Jesus is deviating from the plan. Jesus is likely doing so because he is afraid to take any action which would signal to any spies of the goddess that he had broken their agreement. John reacts by going ahead and performing a baptism on Jesus, but only the first half. Just the drowning part.

The Baptism of John the Baptist

First, we need to remember that John was identified with the prophet Elijah:

11 I tell you the truth: Among those born of women there has not risen anyone greater than John the Baptist; yet he who is least in the Kingdom of Heaven is greater than he.

12 From the days of John the Baptist until now, the Kingdom of Heaven has been forcefully advancing, and forceful men lay hold of it.

13 For all the Prophets and the Law prophesied until John.

14 And if you are willing to accept it, he is the Elijah who was to come.

15 He who has ears, let him hear.
(Mat 11:11-15 NIV)

Elijah is well-known for his miracle of the jar of flour and jug of oil which lasted until the end of a drought.

1 Now Elijah the Tishbite, from Tishbe in Gilead, said to Ahab, "As the LORD, the God of Israel, lives, whom I serve, there will be neither dew nor rain in the next few years except at my word."

2 Then the word of the LORD came to Elijah:

3 "Leave here, turn eastward and hide in the Kerith Ravine, east of the Jordan.

4 You will drink from the brook, and I have ordered the ravens to feed you there."

5 So he did what the LORD had told him. He went to the Kerith Ravine, east of the Jordan, and stayed there.

6 The ravens brought him bread and meat in the morning and bread and meat in the evening, and he drank from the brook.

7 Some time later the brook dried up because there had been no rain in the land.

8 Then the word of the LORD came to him:

9 "Go at once to Zarephath of Sidon and stay there. I have commanded a widow in that place to supply you with food."

10 So he went to Zarephath. When he came to the town gate, a widow was there gathering sticks. He called to her and asked, "Would you bring me a little water in a jar so I may have a drink?"

11 As she was going to get it, he called, "And bring me, please, a piece of bread."

12 "As surely as the LORD your God lives," she replied, "I don't have any bread--only a handful of flour in a jar and a little oil in a jug. I am gathering a few sticks to take home and make a meal for myself and my son, that we may eat it--and die."

13 Elijah said to her, "Don't be afraid. Go home and do as you have said. But first make a small cake of bread for me from what you have and bring it to me, and then make something for yourself and your son.

14 For this is what the LORD, the God of Israel, says: 'The jar of flour will not be used up and the jug of oil will not run dry until the day the LORD gives rain on the land.' "

15 She went away and did as Elijah had told her. So there was food every day for Elijah and for the woman and her family.

16 For the jar of flour was not used up and the jug of oil did not run dry, in keeping with the word of the LORD spoken by Elijah.
(1Ki 17:1-16 NIV)

This can be explained by ergot-infected flour, including the tragic result:

17 Some time later the son of the woman who owned the house became ill. He grew worse and worse, and finally stopped breathing.

18 She said to Elijah, "What do you have against me, man of God? Did you come to remind me of my sin and kill my son?"

19 "Give me your son," Elijah replied. He took him from her arms, carried him to the upper room where he was staying, and laid him on his bed.

20 Then he cried out to the LORD, "O LORD my God, have you brought tragedy also upon this widow I am staying with, by causing her son to die?"

21 Then he stretched himself out on the boy three times and cried to the LORD, "O LORD my God, let this boy's life return to him!"

22 The LORD heard Elijah's cry, and the boy's life returned to him, and he lived.
(1Ki 17:17-22 NIV)

Notice how he cured the boy and then look at the account of Elisha, his successor, attempting to revive another boy who had died:

32 When Elisha reached the house, there was the boy lying dead on his couch.
33 He went in, shut the door on the two of them and prayed to the LORD.
34 Then he got on the bed and lay upon the boy, mouth to mouth, eyes to eyes, hands to hands. As he stretched himself out upon him, the boy's body grew warm.
35 Elisha turned away and walked back and forth in the room and then got on the bed and stretched out upon him once more. The boy sneezed seven times and opened his eyes.
(2Ki 4:32-35 NIV)

Both attempts when merged together read like a description of an early form of mouth-to-mouth resuscitation, especially when combined with:

7 the LORD God formed the man from the dust of the ground and breathed into his nostrils the breath of life, and the man became a living being.
(Gen 2:7 NIV)

I assume that John put the accounts of Elijah and Elisha together with Jehovah breathing life into the nostrils of Adam and (re)discovered a method of artificial resuscitation. John used this knowledge to baptize people, in the sense that he drowned them and then resuscitated them so that they were literally reborn. This was the method John used to wash away a person's sins.

The Baptism of Jesus

John was apparently supposed to come before Jesus in some ceremony and be baptized by him. But Jesus was not following the script, insisting that John baptize him. John does so, bringing him down, back first into the depths of the river, and holding him under until his struggles ceased. Then John lets the body flow away with the current.

10 As Jesus was coming up out of the water, he saw heaven being torn open and the Spirit descending on him like a dove.

11 And a voice came from heaven: "You are my Son, whom I love; with you I am well pleased."

(Mar 1:10-11 NIV)

When the heavens split open, Jesus was sinking into the water looking upward when his father, the angel Gabriel, dove into the water to save him, and then held him while blowing the spirit into his nostrils before screaming out that, "This is my Son, whom I love; with him I am well pleased!"

Jesus is now accompanied by his father. We can perhaps gain some clues as to his identity.

Tested by Satan

12 At once the Spirit sent him out into the desert,

13 and he was in the desert forty days, being tempted by Satan. He was with the wild animals, and angels attended him.

(Mar 1:12-13 NIV)

Mark is very short. It identifies the angel as Satan.

1 Then Jesus was led by the Spirit into the desert to be tempted by the devil.

2 After fasting forty days and forty nights, he was hungry.

3 The tempter came to him and said, "If you are the Son of God, tell these stones to become bread."

4 Jesus answered, "It is written: 'Man does not live on bread alone, but on every word that comes from the mouth of God.' "

5 Then the devil took him to the holy city and had him stand on the highest point of the temple.

6 "If you are the Son of God," he said, "throw yourself down. For it is written: " 'He will command his angels concerning you, and they will lift you up in their hands, so that you will not strike your foot against a stone.' "

7 Jesus answered him, "It is also written: 'Do not put the Lord your God to the test.' "

8 Again, the devil took him to a very high mountain and showed him all the kingdoms of the world and their splendor.

9 "All this I will give you," he said, "if you will bow down and worship me."

10 Jesus said to him, "Away from me, Satan! For it is written: 'Worship the Lord your God, and serve him only.' "

11 Then the devil left him, and angels came and attended him. (Mat 4:1-11 NIV)

Matthew expands on Mark with three tests. The first is to turn stones into bread. First, the text tells us that Jesus had not eaten for forty days and that he was hungry. So it is safe to assume that he asked the 'devil' for something to eat and the challenge was the 'devil's' reply.

This whole exchange brings to mind a couple of verses from Matthew:

9 "Which of you, if his son asks for bread, will give him a stone?

10 Or if he asks for a fish, will give him a snake? (Mat 7:9-10 NIV)

This seems custom designed for this occasion. We know that this is not Satan tempting Jesus, but rather his father, the angel Gabriel. Jesus asks his father for some bread, and his father replies with a stone. Jesus had earlier 'asked' for a fish, which is to say the human avatar of Pisces, but his father gave him a snake, his brother John, who simply drowned Jesus without attempting to revive him.

1 Jesus, full of the Holy Spirit, returned from the Jordan and was led by the Spirit in the desert,

2 where for forty days he was tempted by the devil. He ate nothing during those days, and at the end of them he was hungry.

3 The devil said to him, "If you are the Son of God, tell this stone to become bread."

4 Jesus answered, "It is written: 'Man does not live on bread alone.' "

5 The devil led him up to a high place and showed him in an instant all the kingdoms of the world.

6 And he said to him, "I will give you all their authority and splendor, for it has been given to me, and I can give it to anyone I want to.

7 So if you worship me, it will all be yours."

8 Jesus answered, "It is written: 'Worship the Lord your God and serve him only.' "

9 The devil led him to Jerusalem and had him stand on the highest point of the temple. "If you are the Son of God," he said, "throw yourself down from here.

10 For it is written: " 'He will command his angels concerning you to guard you carefully;

11 they will lift you up in their hands, so that you will not strike your foot against a stone.' "

12 Jesus answered, "It says: 'Do not put the Lord your God to the test.' "

13 When the devil had finished all this tempting, he left him until an opportune time.

(Luk 4:1-13 NIV)

Luke follows Matthew but reverses the second and third tests. In Matthew, the test runs first stone into bread, then to throw himself down from the highest point of the temple and lastly, to worship Satan in return for the authority and splendor of all the world's kingdoms.

We can see the reversal in Luke of the second and third test as an acknowledgment that the two tests are two sides of a single test. He either stands at the highest point of the temple, or he stands high above the earth with authority over all the world's kingdoms. He is being given the choice of priest or king. Jesus' refusal to throw himself down from the temple would seem to indicate that he was OK with the role of priest, but he could not be king, because that would require him to worship his father, the angel who had sex with his mother before whoring her out to others, rather than God.

If that is true, then that would leave the position of king to his brother John. John however then got himself arrested and beheaded.

The Beheading of John

17 For Herod himself had given orders to have John arrested, and he had him bound and put in prison. He did this because of Herodias, his brother Philip's wife, whom he had married.

18 For John had been saying to Herod, "It is not lawful for you to have your brother's wife."

19 So Herodias nursed a grudge against John and wanted to kill him. But she was not able to,

20 because Herod feared John and protected him, knowing him to be a righteous and holy man. When Herod heard John, he was greatly puzzled; yet he liked to listen to him.

21 Finally the opportune time came. On his birthday Herod gave a banquet for his high officials and military commanders and the leading men of Galilee.

22 When the daughter of Herodias came in and danced, she pleased Herod and his dinner guests. The king said to the girl, "Ask me for anything you want, and I'll give it to you."

23 And he promised her with an oath, "Whatever you ask I will give you, up to half my kingdom."

24 She went out and said to her mother, "What shall I ask for?" "The head of John the Baptist," she answered.

25 At once the girl hurried in to the king with the request: "I want you to give me right now the head of John the Baptist on a platter."

26 The king was greatly distressed, but because of his oaths and his dinner guests, he did not want to refuse her.

27 So he immediately sent an executioner with orders to bring John's head. The man went, beheaded John in the prison,

28 and brought back his head on a platter. He presented it to the girl, and she gave it to her mother.

(Mar 6:17-28 NIV)

Mark gives the longer version. In Mark's version, Herod did not want to kill John, it was his wife, Herodias who wanted John dead.

3 Now Herod had arrested John and bound him and put him in prison because of Herodias, his brother Philip's wife,

4 for John had been saying to him: "It is not lawful for you to have her."

5 Herod wanted to kill John, but he was afraid of the people, because they considered him a prophet.

6 On Herod's birthday the daughter of Herodias danced for them and pleased Herod so much

7 that he promised with an oath to give her whatever she asked.

8 Prompted by her mother, she said, "Give me here on a platter the head of John the Baptist."

9 The king was distressed, but because of his oaths and his dinner guests, he ordered that her request be granted

10 and had John beheaded in the prison.

11 His head was brought in on a platter and given to the girl, who carried it to her mother.

(Mat 14:3-11 NIV)

Someone Named Salome

In Matthew's version, it is Herod who wanted John dead, but he was afraid to act because the people considered John to be a prophet. In both versions, the person who gets Herod to act is the daughter of Herodias, who is supposedly never actually named in the Gospels. When I say supposedly never named, there is mention of someone named Salome. The name only occurs in Mark where she is mentioned viewing the crucifixion.

40 Some women were watching from a distance. Among them were Mary Magdalene, Mary the mother of James the younger and of Joses, and Salome.

(Mar 15:40 NIV)

She is also mentioned as being among the group of women who came to anoint his body.

1 When the Sabbath was over, Mary Magdalene, Mary the mother of James, and Salome bought spices so that they might go to anoint Jesus' body.

(Mar 16:1 NIV)

At this point, all we know about Salome is that she was watching the crucifixion with Mary Magdalene and Mary the mother of James the younger and of Joses, but actually, we know that those two Marys are a single person. So there was only Mary and Salome. Then Matthew gets a chance to clear things up:

55 Many women were there, watching from a distance. They had followed Jesus from Galilee to care for his needs.

56 Among them were Mary Magdalene, Mary the mother of James and Joses, and the mother of Zebedee's sons.
(Mat 27:55-56 NIV)

Matthew does not use her name; instead, the Gospel uses its parallel construction with the corresponding verse from Mark to imply that Salome is the mother of Zebedee's sons. Then in the corresponding verse to the one where Salome and Mary go to anoint Jesus, Salome is missing from the narrative:

1 After the Sabbath, at dawn on the first day of the week, Mary Magdalene and the other Mary went to look at the tomb.
(Mat 28:1 NIV)

The Sons of Zebedee

Still, the question we should be asking is who the sons of Zebedee are.

16 As Jesus walked beside the Sea of Galilee, he saw Simon and his brother Andrew casting a net into the lake, for they were fishermen.
17 "Come, follow me," Jesus said, "and I will make you fishers of men."
18 At once they left their nets and followed him.
19 When he had gone a little farther, he saw James son of Zebedee and his brother John in a boat, preparing their nets.
20 Without delay he called them, and they left their father Zebedee in the boat with the hired men and followed him.
(Mar 1:16-20 NIV)

According to the Gospels, James and John are the sons of Zebedee. Zebedee was a fisherman, and according to this line of reasoning, Salome was his wife.

There was also a Salome in the *Protevangelium of James* who did not believe that a virgin could give birth and so she physically checked just after Jesus was born and her hand caught on fire and fell off!

And the midwife cried aloud and said: Great unto me to-day is this day, in that I have seen this new sight. 3 And the midwife went forth of the cave and Salome met her. And she said to her: Salome, Salome, a new sight have I to tell thee. A virgin hath brought forth, which her nature alloweth not. And Salome said: As the Lord my God liveth, if I make not trial and prove her nature I will not believe that a virgin hath brought forth.

XX. 1 And the midwife went in and said unto Mary: Order thyself, for there is no small contention arisen concerning thee. And Salome made trial and cried out and said: Woe unto mine iniquity and mine unbelief, because I have tempted the living God, and lo, my hand falleth away from me in fire. And she bowed her knees unto the Lord, saying: O God of my fathers, remember that I am the seed of Abraham and Isaac and Jacob: make me not a public example unto the children of Israel, but restore me unto the poor, for thou knowest, Lord, that in thy name did I perform my cures, and did receive my hire of thee. 3 And lo, an angel of the Lord appeared, saying unto her: Salome, Salome, the Lord hath hearkened to thee: bring thine hand near unto the young child and take him up, and there shall be unto thee salvation and joy. 4 And Salome came near and took him up, saying: I will do him worship, for a great king is born unto Israel. And behold immediately Salome was healed: and she went forth of the cave justified. And Io, a voice saying: Salome, Salome, tell none of the marvels which thou hast seen, until the child enter into Jerusalem.

This Salome is apparently supposed to be the same as the wife of Zebedee. Imagine the odds of that. The wife of the fisherman whose sons would one day follow Jesus, happened to run into Mary's midwife just after the birth of Jesus and confirmed that her hymen was still intact. This story was still preferable to the other possibility, the same one that Luke makes clear below.

Where Mark and Matthew named some women watching the Crucifixion, Luke is much more discreet:

49 But all those who knew him, including the women who had followed him from Galilee, stood at a distance, watching these things. (Luk 23:49 NIV)

Then when the women go to anoint the body we finally get some names:

1 On the first day of the week, very early in the morning, the women took the spices they had prepared and went to the tomb.

2 They found the stone rolled away from the tomb,

3 but when they entered, they did not find the body of the Lord Jesus.

4 While they were wondering about this, suddenly two men in clothes that gleamed like lightning stood beside them.

5 In their fright the women bowed down with their faces to the ground, but the men said to them, "Why do you look for the living among the dead?

6 He is not here; he has risen! Remember how he told you, while he was still with you in Galilee:

7 'The Son of Man must be delivered into the hands of sinful men, be crucified and on the third day be raised again.' "

8 Then they remembered his words.

9 When they came back from the tomb, they told all these things to the Eleven and to all the others.

10 It was Mary Magdalene, Joanna, Mary the mother of James, and the others with them who told this to the apostles.

(Luk 24:1-10 NIV)

We get a list of Mary Magdalene, Joanna, Mary the mother of James, and unnamed others. Mary Magdalene is identical to Mary the mother of James so that just leaves Joanna. Searching through Luke for another mention of Joanna we find the following verse:

3 Joanna the wife of Cuza, the manager of Herod's household; Susanna; and many others. These women were helping to support them out of their own means.

(Luk 8:3 NIV)

Joanna was the wife of Herod's butler. If Luke states explicitly that someone associated with Herod's personal staff was a follower of Jesus then why should we assume that the Salome mentioned in the Gospels is absolutely not the daughter of Herod's wife with the same name? The Salome who watched the Crucifixion from a distance is no more the mother of Zebedee's children than Mary

Magdalene is another person than Mary, the mother of James and Jose. This has been done to conceal the fact that Salome the daughter of Herodias was a follower of Jesus.

Salome at the Party

It is to this Salome that Jesus says the following at her step-father's birthday party:

Jesus said: Two will rest upon a couch; one will die, the other live.
Salome said: Who are you, man, whose son? You have mounted my couch and eaten from my table.
Jesus said to her: I am he who comes forth from the one who is integrated; I was given of the things of my Father.
<Salome said:> I am your disciple.
<Jesus said to her:> Therefore I say: If he is integrated, he is full of light, but if he is divided, he will be full of darkness.
(GoT 61)

Two will rest on a couch, this seems to be referring to Jesus and Salome, though it may actually be referring to Jesus and John. Jesus is reclining on Salome's couch now, at her father's birthday party. John is also resting on a slab in his cell in prison.

Salome asks who Jesus is, and who his father is.

Jesus answers that he comes from the one who is integrated and that Jesus received the things of his father.

Salome says that she is Jesus' disciple.

Jesus then claims that the one who is integrated is full of light, while a divided person is full of darkness. To correctly understand this last line, we will have to return to the Gospel of Thomas, where we find the following three consecutive sayings that all have to do with vision and/or light: sayings 24, 25, and 26. As a general rule, I prefer to approach groups of sayings in reverse order so we will begin with the last saying in the sequence:

The Beam in your Eye

Jesus said: You see the speck which is in your brother's eye; but you do not see the beam which is in your own eye. When you cast out

*the beam from your own eye, then you will see to cast out the mote
from your brother's eye.*
    (GoT 26)

This saying has to do with the eye, but on a level which we are
not used to thinking of. Traditionally this saying is understood as
having to do with hypocrisy. It supposedly means that we should not
go interfering in other people's lives when we have our own issues
which we should be dealing with. While that is, of course, true, there
is a much deeper level of meaning contained within the saying.

A mote is a speck, a small particle. The original word meant
dried up, withered. So it was referring to a tiny piece of dried up
material, of the same substance as the beam. Let us say that a tiny
particle of sawdust landed on the surface of an eyeball. My wife
once had something in her eye. I looked at it under a bright light, and
I could see a white speck on her eye. I could also, of course, see the
light that was reflected in her eye from the light bulb in the lamp.
However, as I studied the speck of white I saw resting on her lens, I
suddenly realized that what I was seeing was not a foreign object at
all. Instead, it was the light from the light bulb being reflected back
from the surface of my eye and then onto her eye.

The solution is to have a light source that does not shine into the
examiner's eyes. That is why doctors use penlights. They have to
ensure that the beam of light from the light source is not also shining
into their own eyes. This is especially significant to this saying if we
consider the beam to be a two-dimensional line and the mote a one-
dimensional point where the beam of light intersected the reflective
surface of the three-dimensional eye.

The next saying, actually the previous in the usual sequence,
also mentions an eye, and, it too, is really about shielding that eye
from light.

The Apple of your Eye

*Jesus said: Love your brother as your soul; watch over him like
the apple of your eye.*
    (GoT 25)

With this saying, we are told to love our brother as our soul.
That seems clear enough. Then we are to watch over him like the

apple of our eye. This phrase, apple of your eye, occurs in both Proverbs and Psalms. First a look at Proverbs:

2 Keep my commands and you will live; guard my teachings as the apple of your eye.
(Pro 7:2 NIV)

The word translated as apple,' *iyshown* means either 'pupil of the eye' or 'middle of the night' (that is the deepest blackness). Clearly here it is referring to the pupil of the eye. And how does one protect the pupil of one's eye? One shields it from the light. Or as Psalms puts it:

8 Keep me as the apple of your eye; hide me in the shadow of your wings
(Psa 17:8 NIV)

Now we need to realize that when Jesus is using the term 'brother' in these sayings, he is talking about John the Baptist, though they are only half-brothers on their father's side. It is John that Jesus will protect like the apple of his eye, which means he will shield him from the light.

Finally, we get to saying 24:

The Light within a Man of Light

His disciples said: Show us the place where you are, for we must seek it.
He said to them: He who has ears, let him hear!
There is light within a man of light, and he lights the whole world. If he does not enlighten, there is darkness.
(GoT 24)

This saying seems to be based on the emission theory of vision, which was based on the idea that vision was accomplished by beams emitted from the eyes. These beams are made up of streams of invisible probes that originate from the element of fire contained within the eyes. The saying claims that if you want to find Jesus, you must look for the light. This need not be understood as a literal light. It is enough if someone throws new light on old teachings.

Jesus said: Two will rest upon a couch; one will die, the other live.

Salome said: Who are you, man, whose son? You have mounted my couch and eaten from my table.

Jesus said to her: I am he who comes forth from the one who is integrated; I was given of the things of my Father.

<Salome said:> I am your disciple.

<Jesus said to her:> Therefore I say: If he is integrated, he is full of light, but if he is divided, he will be full of darkness.

(GoT 61)

So, let us return to Jesus on Salome's couch. They are at Herod's birthday celebration. Jesus gained entrance because his father posed as a leading man of Galilee. Salome, like her mother Herodias, is a follower of the goddess. Jesus explains to Salome that while he is full of light, his brother is full of darkness. So while Jesus is integrated, a whole man, his brother is divided. Would it not be more fitting if John's physical state corresponded to his divided nature?

21 Finally the opportune time came. On his birthday Herod gave a banquet for his high officials and military commanders and the leading men of Galilee.

22 When the daughter of Herodias came in and danced, she pleased Herod and his dinner guests. The king said to the girl, "Ask me for anything you want, and I'll give it to you."

23 And he promised her with an oath, "Whatever you ask I will give you, up to half my kingdom."

24 She went out and said to her mother, "What shall I ask for?" "The head of John the Baptist," she answered.

25 At once the girl hurried in to the king with the request: "I want you to give me right now the head of John the Baptist on a platter."

26 The king was greatly distressed, but because of his oaths and his dinner guests, he did not want to refuse her.

27 So he immediately sent an executioner with orders to bring John's head. The man went, beheaded John in the prison,

28 and brought back his head on a platter. He presented it to the girl, and she gave it to her mother.

(Mar 6:21-28 NIV)

So, John was beheaded. He is dead and gone from the story. Right? So it would seem.

However, the following section of text from the *Secret Book of James,* the same place where we found the list of the seven key parables, seems to suggest that the 'beheading' might not have been quite what we suppose.

John and the Head of Prophecy

Then I asked him, "Master, can we prophesy to those who ask us to prophesy to them? There are many who bring a request to us and look to us to hear our pronouncement."

The master answered and said, "Do you not know that the head of prophecy was cut off with John?"

But I said, "Master, is it not impossible to remove the head of prophecy?"

The master said to me, "When you realize what 'head' means, and that prophecy comes from the head, then understand the meaning of 'its head was removed.'

"First I spoke with you in parables, and you did not understand. Now I am speaking with you openly, and you do not grasp it. Nevertheless, you were for me a parable among parables and a disclosure among things revealed.

"Be eager to be saved without being urged. Rather, be fervent on your own and, if possible, outdo even me, for this is how the father will love you.

"Come to hate hypocrisy and evil intention. Intention produces hypocrisy, and hypocrisy is far from truth.

"Do not let the Kingdom of Heaven wither away. It is like a palm shoot whose dates dropped around it. It produced buds, and after they grew, its productivity dried up. This is also what happened with fruit that came from this single root. After it was harvested, fruit was obtained by many. It certainly was good. Is it not possible to produce the new growth now, and for you to find it?

(ApoJ)

The text claims that the head of prophecy was removed with John. Then it explains that when we realize what the word 'head' means and that prophecy comes from this head, we will understand what is meant by how it was removed 'its head was removed.' Then the text says that Jesus used to explain things in parables, but you did not understand so now he is speaking plainly, but you still do not get it. Still, you served as a parable and helped to reveal things that were disclosed. Then a couple more lines of distraction until finally closing on the bit about the palm shoot dropping dates. Let us check out the piece if we remove the bits of misdirection written into the text.

> *Then I asked him, "Master, can we prophesy to those who ask us to prophesy to them? There are many who bring a request to us and look to us to hear our pronouncement."*
>
> *The master answered and said, "Do you not know that the head of prophecy was cut off with John?"*
>
> *But I said, "Master, is it not impossible to remove the head of prophecy?"*
>
> *The master said to me, "When you realize what 'head' means, and that prophecy comes from the head, then understand the meaning of 'its head was removed.'*
>
> *...*
>
> *"Do not let the Kingdom of Heaven wither away. It is like a palm shoot whose dates dropped around it. It produced buds, and after they grew, its productivity dried up. This is also what happened with fruit that came from this single root. After it was harvested, fruit was obtained by many. It certainly was good. Is it not possible to produce the new growth now, and for you to find it?*
>
> *(ApoJ)*

Now it is much clearer that the bit about the palm shoot is connected to the head of prophecy. This palm shoot spreads dates which turn into new plants. Then its productivity ends. The same thing happens to the new plants which grow from the fruit, and this fruit is enjoyed by many. So the text is talking about the life-cycle of a date palm, however, a date palm that has only a single harvest in its life-cycle. Remember however that we are supposed to find the meaning of 'head.' Notice the terms used: 'palm shoot' and 'fruit that comes from this single root.' The whole description reads as being very phallic, with the palm shoot dropping dates, which in this instance is another way of saying 'spilling seed.'

Suppose that the head of prophecy had nothing to do with the head at all. It was more about a single root that spread seed. The head on the silver platter that Salome gave her mother was actually the castrated manhood of John the Baptist. Jesus' debt had been paid.

What happened to John then?

The Secret Gospel of Mark

There is a controversial bit of text known as the Secret Gospel of Mark. The story surrounding it is fascinating as it was supposedly part of a letter written by the Alexandrian Church Father Clement. It describes a section of text which existed in a secret, more spiritual version of the Gospel of Mark. The text below is supposed to have been placed between Mark 10:34 and 35.

And they come into Bethany. And a certain woman whose brother had died was there. And, coming, she prostrated herself before Jesus and says to him, "Son of David, have mercy on me." But the disciples rebuked her. And Jesus, being angered, went off with her into the garden where the tomb was, and straightway a great cry was heard from the tomb. And going near Jesus rolled away the stone from the door of the tomb. And straightway, going in where the youth was, he stretched forth his hand and raised him, seizing his hand. But the youth, looking upon him, loved him and began to beseech him that he might be with him. And going out of the tomb they came into the house of the youth, for he was rich. And after six days Jesus told him what to do and in the evening the youth comes to him, wearing a linen cloth over his naked body. And he remained with him that night, for Jesus taught him the mystery of the kingdom of God. And thence, arising, he returned to the other side of the Jordan.

For me, regardless of where it was found in the Secret Gospel of Mark, the events it describes take place after Jesus is baptized and before he meets up with Simon, Andrew, and the sons of Zebedee. The particular woman whose brother has died is Mary, as John is her half-brother in that they both had the same father. The disciples rebuking her is part of a formula found in Mark and repeated whenever someone comes to 'bother' Jesus or in one case, to waste money on aromatic oil. That being the case, I do not consider that detail to be evidence that the events described could not actually have occurred much earlier in the narrative.

The section from Secret Mark is likely describing the same events that are found in John's story of the raising of Lazarus. Again, this is not to say that these events actually took place in the real world. I do not consider the Gospels to document actual historical events. There may be some factual basis or parallels, but for me, they are primarily literary documents. These documents have however been written in such a way as to have an overt message and a much different covert one.

One method the Gospels use to conceal the hidden message is to split characters into separate individuals. This is how Mary the mother of Jesus was split from Mary Magdalene. This trick is used repeatedly. Whenever there are different individuals with the same name, they are, in nearly every case, the same individual. For instance, let us take James the Great. He is supposedly different than James, the son of Alphaeus (James the Less) and James the brother of Jesus (James the Just). This might make sense if the Gospels were in fact primarily historical documents, recording events that actually took place. However, as I have attempted to demonstrate, the Gospels are something else entirely. They are documents designed to carry both an outer and an inner meaning. One way to do that is to create a variety of separate characters from a single character and to juggle a variety of designations that require one to be a scholar to keep all of these identities straight.

So the person known as John the Baptist was not beheaded. He was instead castrated. This was brought about by Herodias who was a follower of the goddess together with her daughter Salome. Jesus gave Salome the go-ahead when he appeared at Herod's birthday celebration. John became Jesus' unwitting redeemer. John ended up paying ransom for Jesus, a payment that came due when Jesus learned the secrets of the goddess and was finally settled by an unsuspecting John.

Mary then came to Jesus and begged him to save her brother. Jesus went to the tomb where John had been locked away to suffer and eventually die from his untreated wound. Jesus had the stone rolled back and treated John, who almost certainly had no idea at that time that Jesus had betrayed him. Jesus applied the medical knowledge he had learned when with the followers of the goddess and treated John's wounds as well as instructing him in the secret teachings before leaving him. Still, they were destined to meet again.

16 As Jesus walked beside the Sea of Galilee, he saw Simon and his brother Andrew casting a net into the lake, for they were fishermen.

17 "Come, follow me," Jesus said, "and I will make you fishers of men."

18 At once they left their nets and followed him.

19 When he had gone a little farther, he saw James son of Zebedee and his brother John in a boat, preparing their nets.

20 Without delay he called them, and they left their father Zebedee in the boat with the hired men and followed him.

(Mar 1:16-20 NIV)

Great, here we have Jesus walking along the Sea of Galilee when he sees Simon and his brother, Andrew, fishing. Jesus tells them to follow him, and then they run across John and James, the sons of Zebedee in a boat and Jesus calls them too. So they leave their father in the boat and follow Jesus. Notice how the text makes it very clear that John and James leave their father there in the boat. It almost seems as though this was written specifically to counter any claims that their father might not have been left behind at all.

18 As Jesus was walking beside the Sea of Galilee, he saw two brothers, Simon called Peter and his brother Andrew. They were casting a net into the lake, for they were fishermen.

19 "Come, follow me," Jesus said, "and I will make you fishers of men."

20 At once they left their nets and followed him.

21 Going on from there, he saw two other brothers, James son of Zebedee and his brother John. They were in a boat with their father Zebedee, preparing their nets. Jesus called them,

22 and immediately they left the boat and their father and followed him.

(Mat 4:18-22 NIV)

Matthew follows Mark quite closely and once again makes it crystal clear that James and John leave their father behind on his boat.

3 He got into one of the boats, the one belonging to Simon, and asked him to put out a little from shore. Then he sat down and taught the people from the boat.

4 When he had finished speaking, he said to Simon, "Put out into deep water, and let down the nets for a catch."

5 Simon answered, "Master, we've worked hard all night and haven't caught anything. But because you say so, I will let down the nets."

6 When they had done so, they caught such a large number of fish that their nets began to break.

7 So they signaled their partners in the other boat to come and help them, and they came and filled both boats so full that they began to sink.

8 When Simon Peter saw this, he fell at Jesus' knees and said, "Go away from me, Lord; I am a sinful man!"

9 For he and all his companions were astonished at the catch of fish they had taken,

10 and so were James and John, the sons of Zebedee, Simon's partners. Then Jesus said to Simon, "Don't be afraid; from now on you will catch men."

11 So they pulled their boats up on shore, left everything and followed him.

(Luk 5:3-11 NIV)

Luke makes the whole event rather fantastic, with Jesus helping them to catch so many fish that the boats begin to sink. However, the chief difference between Luke and the others is that in Luke, Jesus already knows Simon. In Mark and Matthew meeting Simon and Andrew was the first thing Jesus did after returning from the desert after being tempted by the devil. In Luke, however, Jesus first taught at a few synagogues and threw out a demon before visiting Simon's house:

38 Jesus left the synagogue and went to the home of Simon. Now Simon's mother-in-law was suffering from a high fever, and they asked Jesus to help her.

39 So he bent over her and rebuked the fever, and it left her. She got up at once and began to wait on them.

(Luk 4:38-39 NIV)

So, in Luke, Jesus knew Simon before he found him in his fishing boat with his brother Andrew. And what were they doing, really, in that fishing boat? Jesus says that he will make them fishers of men, but what if that is what they already were? Suppose that the term 'fish' does not mean a literal fish but rather a type of person. Consider the following miracle from Matthew:

24 After Jesus and his disciples arrived in Capernaum, the collectors of the two-drachma tax came to Peter and asked, "Doesn't your teacher pay the temple tax?"
25 "Yes, he does," he replied. When Peter came into the house, Jesus was the first to speak. "What do you think, Simon?" he asked. "From whom do the kings of the earth collect duty and taxes--from their own sons or from others?"
26 "From others," Peter answered. "Then the sons are exempt," Jesus said to him.
27 "But so that we may not offend them, go to the lake and throw out your line. Take the first fish you catch; open its mouth and you will find a four-drachma coin. Take it and give it to them for my tax and yours."
(Mat 17:24-27 NIV)

Rather than Simon casting a line in the sea, suppose that Jesus was actually telling Simon to go and perform before an audience until a person gullible enough to cough up four drachmas is found. This is the fish Simon and his brother are fishing for, followers with coin, ready to be seduced by miracles and mystical teachings.

Remember that Jesus met John in the Jordan River which runs through the Sea of Galilee. Here we have Jesus meeting Simon and Andrew in one boat and then John and James in the next. Also, an important point to keep in mind is that Mark and Matthew both say 'James son of Zebedee and his brother John' while Luke calls them 'James and John, the sons of Zebedee' which is a significant difference. The difference being James and John might have different fathers but share a mother. The wording in Matthew and Mark would seem to point to such a possibility while Luke makes it clear that they have the same father. And who would this father be? According to what I see as the hidden reading, John being John the Baptist has the angel Gabriel as a father while James being the brother of Jesus again has Gabriel for a father. Zebedee seems to be a cipher for the angel Gabriel.

That being the case, the angel is right there, in the boat. We should be able to identify him. All three of the Synoptic Gospels agree that they, John and James, left their father behind. Again what is interesting is how they make a point to do so, so that there can be no misunderstanding. John and James left Zebedee their father behind in the boat and followed Jesus. But what that shows is that someone had argued in the past that Zebedee had not been left behind at all. But who could it be?

The only other people around were Simon and Andrew. There is not much written about Andrew except in the gospel of John which I generally ignore. We can now consider afresh why it is that I find John to be untrustworthy when constructing the hidden Thomasine narrative. It is simply that there is only one John. John the Baptist is identical with John the Apostle and John the Evangelist. John, once the truth behind his castration was revealed, became decidedly antagonist towards anything that would lead to uncovering the hidden teachings of Jesus, because he hoped to eliminate everything having to do with his brother's secret plans and knowledge.

John's castration turned him away from the material world, where he had initially been chosen by his father to found a dynasty of seafaring explorers. Instead, he founded a spiritual order opposed to the material realm. He created his gospel, together with his revelation to mislead the ignorant and to ensnare the true seekers within paradoxical labyrinths where the quest for truth inevitably devolves into the battle of Armageddon.

I am not claiming that one person actually wrote all the books bearing John's name. I am only stating what I believe the hidden narrative is indicating. My own feeling is that all of the books bearing John's name were written by one community or school of thought.

Andrew has a few things written about him, but as they only occur with the gospel of John they can be discounted as having anything to do with the hidden narrative. That just leaves us with Simon. If we keep to our one name per individual then clearly the Simon that Jesus meets in the Sea of Galilee is actually Simon, his brother. This does not mean that Simon could not also be the angel Gabriel in disguise because, as Mary was Jesus' sister as well as mother, if Gabriel were considered Mary's husband then he would be Jesus' brother-in-law in addition to being his father.

The Many Simons of the Synoptic Gospels

Ok, so exactly how many characters named Simon are there in the Synoptic Gospels?

First, there is Simon Peter, then Simon the Zealot also known as Simon the Canaanite:

4 Simon the Zealot and Judas Iscariot, who betrayed him.
(Mat 10:4 NIV)

Then there is Simon, the brother of Jesus:

3 Isn't this the carpenter? Isn't this Mary's son and the brother of James, Joseph, Judas and Simon? Aren't his sisters here with us?"
And they took offense at him.
(Mar 6:3 NIV)

Then there is Simon, the leper:

3 While he was in Bethany, reclining at the table in the home of a man known as Simon the Leper, a woman came with an alabaster jar of very expensive perfume, made of pure nard. She broke the jar and poured the perfume on his head.
(Mar 14:3 NIV)

Then there is another Simon, this time he is a Pharisee:

36 Now one of the Pharisees invited Jesus to have dinner with him, so he went to the Pharisee's house and reclined at the table.
37 When a woman who had lived a sinful life in that town learned that Jesus was eating at the Pharisee's house, she brought an alabaster jar of perfume,
38 and as she stood behind him at his feet weeping, she began to wet his feet with her tears. Then she wiped them with her hair, kissed them and poured perfume on them.

39 When the Pharisee who had invited him saw this, he said to himself, "If this man were a prophet, he would know who is touching him and what kind of woman she is--that she is a sinner."

40 Jesus answered him, "Simon, I have something to tell you." "Tell me, teacher," he said.

(Luk 7:36-40 NIV)

Finally, there was Simon the Cyrenian:

32 As they were going out, they met a man from Cyrene, named Simon, and they forced him to carry the cross.

(Mat 27:32 NIV)

Again, my claim is simple. Simon Peter, Simon the Zealot, Simon the brother of Jesus, Simon the leper, Simon the Pharisee, and Simon the Cyrenian are all the same individual. However, there is also a Simeon mentioned in Luke and Simeon is merely another form of Simon. Simeon was, as you will recall, the man who met Mary, Joseph, and Jesus when they entered the Temple for the presentation of Jesus at the Temple. The text concerning the event found within Luke was written in such a way as to suggest that this Simeon was the officiating priest. This is especially significant when we consider how Jesus replied to his mother's words when he was found at the temple in Jerusalem after going missing when he was twelve:

48 When his parents saw him, they were astonished. His mother said to him, "Son, why have you treated us like this? Your father and I have been anxiously searching for you."

49 "Why were you searching for me?" he asked. "Didn't you know I had to be in my Father's house?"

(Luk 2:48-49 NIV)

Could it be possible that the angel Gabriel was identical with not just Simeon the priest, but with Simon Peter himself? Let us look at some verses that might help illuminate how Jesus saw Simon Peter. The first verse that we are going to look at, we just discussed above. Still, it will be helpful to examine it again:

24 After Jesus and his disciples arrived in Capernaum, the collectors of the two-drachma tax came to Peter and asked, "Doesn't your teacher pay the temple tax?"

25 "Yes, he does," he replied. When Peter came into the house, Jesus was the first to speak. "What do you think, Simon?" he asked. "From whom do the kings of the earth collect duty and taxes--from their own sons or from others?"

26 "From others," Peter answered. "Then the sons are exempt," Jesus said to him.

27 "But so that we may not offend them, go to the lake and throw out your line. Take the first fish you catch; open its mouth and you will find a four-drachma coin. Take it and give it to them for my tax and yours."
(Mat 17:24-27 NIV)

Before we were concerned with the fish and the coin found in its mouth. This time I want to focus on the question Jesus asks Simon: "From whom do the kings of the earth collect duty and taxes--from their own sons or from others?" Here the question takes on a double meaning. If Simon is actually the father of Jesus and if he has come to Jesus to collect the tax, then he has, in fact, come to collect the tax from his son.

Simon as the Adversary

31 He then began to teach them that the Son of Man must suffer many things and be rejected by the elders, chief priests and teachers of the law, and that he must be killed and after three days rise again.

32 He spoke plainly about this, and Peter took him aside and began to rebuke him.

33 But when Jesus turned and looked at his disciples, he rebuked Peter. "Get behind me, Satan!" he said. "You do not have in mind the things of God, but the things of men."
(Mar 8:31-33 NIV)

21 From that time on Jesus began to explain to his disciples that he must go to Jerusalem and suffer many things at the hands of the elders, chief priests and teachers of the law, and that he must be killed and on the third day be raised to life.

22 Peter took him aside and began to rebuke him. "Never, Lord!" he said. "This shall never happen to you!"

23 Jesus turned and said to Peter, "Get behind me, Satan! You are a stumbling block to me; you do not have in mind the things of God, but the things of men."

(Mat 16:21-23 NIV)

In the selections from Mark and Matthew above we have Jesus comparing Simon Peter to Satan. This brings us back to when Jesus was being tempted by the devil after being baptized by John:

10 Jesus said to him, "Away from me, Satan! For it is written: 'Worship the Lord your God, and serve him only.' "

(Mat 4:10 NIV)

As I have stated, Jesus was actually being tested by his father, the angel Gabriel. Here we see Jesus using the same name for Simon Peter. Coincidence, or is it by design?

Father is Thirsty

32 They went to a place called Gethsemane, and Jesus said to his disciples, "Sit here while I pray."

33 He took Peter, James and John along with him, and he began to be deeply distressed and troubled.

34 "My soul is overwhelmed with sorrow to the point of death," he said to them. "Stay here and keep watch."

35 Going a little farther, he fell to the ground and prayed that if possible the hour might pass from him.

36 "Abba, Father," he said, "everything is possible for you. Take this cup from me. Yet not what I will, but what you will."

37 Then he returned to his disciples and found them sleeping. "Simon," he said to Peter, "are you asleep? Could you not keep watch for one hour?

38 Watch and pray so that you will not fall into temptation. The spirit is willing, but the body is weak."

39 Once more he went away and prayed the same thing.

40 When he came back, he again found them sleeping, because their eyes were heavy. They did not know what to say to him.

41 Returning the third time, he said to them, "Are you still sleeping and resting? Enough! The hour has come. Look, the Son of Man is betrayed into the hands of sinners.
(Mar 14:32-41 NIV)

In the section above from Mark, we have what is called the Agony in the Garden. Look at it from what we know about the sacred bread. Eating the bread would keep one awake while drinking wine would put one to sleep. Jesus has eaten the bread, and he is awake on all levels, but he also has a goblet of wine, which will counteract the effects of the bread and put the person who drinks it asleep.

Jesus says: "Abba, Father," he said, "everything is possible for you. Take this cup from me. Yet not what I will, but what you will."

In the traditional reading, this is Jesus praying to God, his father in heaven, that he might remove this bitter destiny that is about to unfold. In our new reading, this is Jesus talking to his father Simon Peter who comes to take the goblet of wine.

36 Then Jesus went with his disciples to a place called Gethsemane, and he said to them, "Sit here while I go over there and pray."

37 He took Peter and the two sons of Zebedee along with him, and he began to be sorrowful and troubled.

38 Then he said to them, "My soul is overwhelmed with sorrow to the point of death. Stay here and keep watch with me."

39 Going a little farther, he fell with his face to the ground and prayed, "My Father, if it is possible, may this cup be taken from me. Yet not as I will, but as you will."

40 Then he returned to his disciples and found them sleeping. "Could you men not keep watch with me for one hour?" he asked Peter.

41 "Watch and pray so that you will not fall into temptation. The spirit is willing, but the body is weak."

42 He went away a second time and prayed, "My Father, if it is not possible for this cup to be taken away unless I drink it, may your will be done."

43 When he came back, he again found them sleeping, because their eyes were heavy.

44 So he left them and went away once more and prayed the third time, saying the same thing.

45 Then he returned to the disciples and said to them, "Are you still sleeping and resting? Look, the hour is near, and the Son of Man is betrayed into the hands of sinners.

(Mat 26:36-45 NIV)

In Matthew above we see it play out over and over. The first time Jesus asks his father to take the cup from him if that is what he wills. Then Jesus finds the disciples are sleeping. He asks Peter why they could not stay awake for one hour. Jesus tells them to watch and pray. Then he prays again to his father, that if his father insists that he will not take the cup away from Jesus unless Jesus first drinks from it, Jesus understands. It would seem that in each case his father was more than willing to take the cup of wine from Jesus before he drank from it.

39 Jesus went out as usual to the Mount of Olives, and his disciples followed him.

40 On reaching the place, he said to them, "Pray that you will not fall into temptation."

41 He withdrew about a stone's throw beyond them, knelt down and prayed,

42 "Father, if you are willing, take this cup from me; yet not my will, but yours be done."

43 An angel from heaven appeared to him and strengthened him.

44 And being in anguish, he prayed more earnestly, and his sweat was like drops of blood falling to the ground.

45 When he rose from prayer and went back to the disciples, he found them asleep, exhausted from sorrow.

46 "Why are you sleeping?" he asked them. "Get up and pray so that you will not fall into temptation."

(Luk 22:39-46 NIV)

Finally, we have the version from Luke where once Jesus asks his father to take the cup an angel appears gives Jesus strength. This is just Gabriel, in his guise of Simon Peter come to take the goblet of wine from Jesus. The sweat like drops of blood is again supposed to remind us of the wine. And once again the disciples fall asleep because they have drunk from Jesus' cup.

Is Simon really the angel who first appeared to Anna, the mother of Mary? Looking back at the events from the *Protevangelium of James,* let us return to the discussion between Anna and her handmaiden:

II. 2 And the great day of the Lord drew nigh, and Judith her handmaid said unto her: How long humblest thou thy soul? The great day of the Lord hath come, and it is not lawful for thee to mourn: but take this headband, which the mistress of my work gave me, and it is not lawful for me to put it on, forasmuch as I am an handmaid, and it hath a mark of royalty. And Anna said: Get thee from me. Lo! I have done nothing (or I will not do so) and the Lord hath greatly humbled me: peradventure one gave it to thee in subtlety, and thou art come to make me partaker in thy sin. And Judith said: How shall I curse thee, seeing the Lord hath shut up thy womb, to give thee no fruit in Israel?

Judith: a Daughter of Simeon

My understanding is that the handmaiden being named Judith is not an accident. There is an apocryphal, deuterocanonical book called the Book of Judith which is included in the Septuagint and the Catholic Bibles. It is the story of Judith, a widow, who, accompanied by her handmaiden, goes to the camp of the enemy and tricks the general, Holofernes, by promising to provide him with information on the Israelites. Gaining his trust, she is allowed into his tent one night where he has collapsed in a drunken stupor. She then beheads him and saves Israel.

1 Judith fell upon her face, and put ashes upon her head, and uncovered the sackcloth wherewith she was clothed; and about the time that the incense of that evening was offered in Jerusalem in the house of the Lord Judith cried with a loud voice, and said,
2 O Lord God of my father Simeon, to whom thou gavest a sword to take vengeance of the strangers, who loosened the girdle of a maid to defile her, and discovered the thigh to her shame, and polluted her virginity to her reproach; for thou saidst, It shall not be so; and yet they did so:

3 Wherefore thou gavest their rulers to be slain, so that they dyed their bed in blood, being deceived, and smotest the servants with their lords, and the lords upon their thrones;

4 And hast given their wives for a prey, and their daughters to be captives, and all their spoils to be divided among thy dear children; which were moved with thy zeal, and abhorred the pollution of their blood, and called upon thee for aid: O God, O my God, hear me also a widow.

(Jdt 9:1-4 KJA)

Judith calls for vengeance by recalling the bloody actions of her father Simeon, when he and Levi slaughtered all the men of a city after one of its inhabitants, Shechem, raped Dinah, one of Simeon and Levi's sisters. Judith seems to be claiming that she a member of the lost and scattered tribe of Simeon. And now we have Anna's handmaiden, who is named Judith, giving Anna a royal headband which she then wears as she draws down the angel Gabriel, who takes the human form of a man named Simon.

It almost seems as though the angel had had his eyes on Anna for a while and was just waiting for an opportunity to breach the wall between the angelic and the mundane. And then he used Judith to deliver the ceremonial headband to Anna.

The Righteous Angel

More threads ti Peter Simon to an angel interfering in the world of men. Consider, for instance, one of the most enigmatic of sayings from the Gospel of Thomas:

Jesus said to his disciples: Compare me, tell me whom I am like. Simon Peter said to him: You are like a righteous angel. Matthew said to him: You are like a wise philosopher. Thomas said to him: Master, my mouth is wholly incapable of saying whom you are like. Jesus said: I am not your master, for you have drunk, and have become drunk from the bubbling spring which I have caused to gush forth. And he took him, withdrew, telling him three words. Now when Thomas returned to his companions, they asked him: What did Jesus say to you? Thomas said to them: If I tell you one of the words which he said to me, you will take up stones and throw them at me; and a fire will come out of the stones and burn you up.

145

(GoT 13)

One technique I apply to difficult sayings like this is to read two consecutive sayings as a single unit, beginning with the latter member of the pair in the collection. So basically we should read 14 first and then number 13. I am not going to rearrange them in this instance as I trust the reader will be able to perform the necessary mental gymnastics.

Jesus said to them, "If you fast, you will acquire a sin, and if you pray you will be condemned, and if you give alms, it is evil that you will do unto your spirits. And when you go into any land and travel in the country places, when they receive you eat whatever they serve to you. Heal those among them who are sick. For, nothing that enters your mouth will defile you. Rather, it is precisely what comes out of your mouth that will defile you."
(GoT 14)

When read like this, we can see correspondences between the descriptions the disciples make of Jesus and the various activities. Jesus had never fasted because to do so would be to acquire a sin, and he is seen as a righteous angel. He never prayed because to do so would be to condemn him, and he is seen as a wise philosopher. And he never gave alms because he is seen as something which Thomas is unable to name. Thomas drank from the spring which Jesus brought forth because that is what one does, one consumes what one is served. Jesus tells him, 'Help sick people,' but Thomas knows not to tell the others that because it is not what goes in the mouth but what comes out that is important.

Such an exercise does help to explore the meaning of number 13, but there is a deeper key. It is hidden in the Gospel of Philip. I have reproduced it below with saying 13 from the Gospel of Thomas directly following:

Jesus took them all by stealth, for he did not appear as he was, but in the manner in which they would be able to see him. He appeared to them all. He appeared to the great as great. He appeared to the small as small. He appeared to the angels as an angel, and to men as a man. Because of this, his word hid itself from everyone. Some indeed saw him, thinking that they were seeing

themselves, but when he appeared to his disciples in glory on the mount, he was not small. He became great, but he made the disciples great, that they might be able to see him in his greatness.
(GoPh 29)

Jesus said to his disciples: Compare me, tell me whom I am like. Simon Peter said to him: You are like a righteous angel. Matthew said to him: You are like a wise philosopher. Thomas said to him: Master, my mouth is wholly incapable of saying whom you are like. Jesus said: I am not your master, for you have drunk, and have become drunk from the bubbling spring which I have caused to gush forth. And he took him, withdrew, telling him three words. Now when Thomas returned to his companions, they asked him: What did Jesus say to you? Thomas said to them: If I tell you one of the words which he said to me, you will take up stones and throw them at me; and a fire will come out of the stones and burn you up.
(GoT 13)

Read in light of the section from the Gospel of Philip, Simon Peter seeing Jesus as a righteous angel literally means that Simon Peter is, in reality, a righteous angel. Matthew seeing Jesus as a wise philosopher would seem to suggest that the disciple was, in fact, a philosopher. Is there anything to back this up?

The Wise Philosopher

There is a text titled, *The Book of Thomas the Contender* (Turner), which begins with the following:

The secret words that the savior spoke to Judas Thomas which I, even I, Mathaias, wrote down, while I was walking, listening to them speak with one another.

The opening sentence above makes it clear that this text is to be understood as having been written by Mattaias, or rather the disciple Matthew. The section below makes it clear that the author is familiar with Plato's Allegory of the Cave, even if he takes it in a more apocalyptic direction:

"Woe to you, captives, for you are bound in caverns! You laugh! In mad laughter you rejoice! You neither realize your perdition, nor do you reflect on your circumstances, nor have you understood that you dwell in darkness and death! On the contrary, you are drunk with the fire and full of bitterness. Your mind is deranged on account of the burning that is in you, and sweet to you are the poison and the blows of your enemies! And the darkness rose for you like the light, for you surrendered your freedom for servitude! You darkened your hearts and surrendered your thoughts to folly, and you filled your thoughts with the smoke of the fire that is in you! And your light has hidden in the cloud of [...] and the garment that is put upon you, you [...]. And you were seized by the hope that does not exist. And whom is it you have believed? Do you not know that you all dwell among those who that [...] you as though you [...]. You baptized your souls in the water of darkness! You walked by your own whims!"

This helps to answer one question that has remained unanswered since our discussion of the genealogy of Jesus, which is what the character of the bloodline labeled with the name Matthew was. The name enters the genealogy after Nathan, the son of David, which puts the date around 950 BC which is about three hundred years before the Pre-Socratic philosophers indicating some unknown early Hebrew lover of wisdom, of which there is a rich tradition. The position within the genealogy would place it as the next generation after Solomon, the wise. And so we have a bloodline, not of a single philosopher, but added to by the latest and brightest thinker, generation after generation, perhaps including genetic contributions by Socrates, Plato, and Aristotle.

The next feature of saying 13 which demands our attention is the description offered by Thomas who says that he is incapable of giving a description of Jesus. This is because Thomas, as the twin, is himself already a reflection of Jesus. If anyone who looks at Jesus sees a reflection of themselves, then someone who is already a reflection of Jesus is only going to an infinite regression of empty frames.

Fiery Stones

Finally, we come to the sayings enigmatic conclusion. Thomas claims that if he tells the others even one of the three words which

Jesus said to him that they pick up stones and throw them and from the stones will come fire and burn them up. That is a very distinctive image, fire coming out of stones to burn up those who had thrown them. It got me to wondering how many times stones are mentioned together with fire in the Bible. I thought that maybe the author of Thomas was trying to send an encoded message of sorts. It turns out the words translated as 'fire' and 'stones' occur together in only one section of text where we find the keywords translated as 'fiery stones':

11 The word of the LORD came to me:

12 "Son of man, take up a lament concerning the king of Tyre and say to him: 'This is what the Sovereign LORD says: " 'You were the model of perfection, full of wisdom and perfect in beauty.

13 You were in Eden, the garden of God; every precious stone adorned you: ruby, topaz and emerald, chrysolite, onyx and jasper, sapphire, turquoise and beryl. Your settings and mountings were made of gold; on the day you were created they were prepared.

14 You were anointed as a guardian cherub, for so I ordained you. You were on the holy mount of God; you walked among the fiery stones.

15 You were blameless in your ways from the day you were created till wickedness was found in you.

16 Through your widespread trade you were filled with violence, and you sinned. So I drove you in disgrace from the mount of God, and I expelled you, O guardian cherub, from among the fiery stones.

17 Your heart became proud on account of your beauty, and you corrupted your wisdom because of your splendor. So I threw you to the earth; I made a spectacle of you before kings.

18 By your many sins and dishonest trade you have desecrated your sanctuaries. So I made a fire come out from you, and it consumed you, and I reduced you to ashes on the ground in the sight of all who were watching.

19 All the nations who knew you are appalled at you; you have come to a horrible end and will be no more.' "
(Eze 28:11-19 NIV)

This would seem to be directed to Simon Peter or rather to the angel that stands behind the mask. He was once a guardian angel, but then wickedness was found in him. His business filled him with violence, and he sinned. It is he who will be burnt up from the fire within, but only if Thomas utters the word 'angel' and a stone is hurled to silence the truth.

Still, there is more. Everything above is fine, but it exists solely within apocryphal texts. Without confirmation from within the canonical texts, it means nothing. That is the key, to find something within the Synoptic Gospels that shows that the authors had in mind the various hidden identifies of the disciples as I have indicated here. Namely that John the Baptist is the same as John son of Zebedee and that Simon Peter was an angel, which really means one of the Elohim.

The place where we will find this confirmation is identified in the same section from the *Gospel of Philip* that provided the key to saying number 13:

Jesus took them all by stealth, for he did not appear as he was, but in the manner in which they would be able to see him. He appeared to them all. He appeared to the great as great. He appeared to the small as small. He appeared to the angels as an angel, and to men as a man. Because of this, his word hid itself from everyone. Some indeed saw him, thinking that they were seeing themselves, but when he appeared to his disciples in glory on the mount, he was not small. He became great, but he made the disciples great, that they might be able to see him in his greatness.
(GoPh 29)

On the Mountain of Transfiguration

The text tells us exactly where to look: 'when he appeared to his disciples in glory on the mount.' This is an explicit reference to the events on the mountain of transfiguration:

1 And he said to them, "I tell you the truth, some who are standing here will not taste death before they see the kingdom of God come with power."
2 After six days Jesus took Peter, James and John with him and led them up a high mountain, where they were all alone. There he was transfigured before them.

3 His clothes became dazzling white, whiter than anyone in the world could bleach them.

4 And there appeared before them Elijah and Moses, who were talking with Jesus.

5 Peter said to Jesus, "Rabbi, it is good for us to be here. Let us put up three shelters--one for you, one for Moses and one for Elijah."

6 (He did not know what to say, they were so frightened.)

7 Then a cloud appeared and enveloped them, and a voice came from the cloud: "This is my Son, whom I love. Listen to him!"

8 Suddenly, when they looked around, they no longer saw anyone with them except Jesus.

9 As they were coming down the mountain, Jesus gave them orders not to tell anyone what they had seen until the Son of Man had risen from the dead.

10 They kept the matter to themselves, discussing what "rising from the dead" meant.

(Mar 9:1-10 NIV)

Above is the version from Mark. Note the full cast of characters: Jesus takes with him James, John, and Peter. On the mountain, they encounter Moses, Elijah, and a cloud from which comes a voice. James represented the Law of Moses, John was seen as Elijah reborn, and Peter was actually an angel, one definition of which was simply, messenger. Jesus says that some who are standing will not die until they see the kingdom come with power, then he takes James, John, and Peter up the mountain where he reveals his semi-angelic nature, John steps into the role of Elijah: prophet and miracle worker. James becomes Moses: lawgiver and law-preserver. Peter hides within his tent which he fills with mist so that he can unveil his angelic nature and clasp the crown of Jehovah for himself. Indeed the kingdom has come in power as the renegade Elohim leads his semi-divine sons, his band of brothers and half-brothers, down the mountain and into history.

But who is Jesus? He alone does not have a preexistent archetype to step into.

First, we should look at where Moses and Elijah stood in the cosmic framework. During the age of Aries, the planet that ruled Aries was Mars. Mars also ruled the sign Scorpio, which was the age's counter-sign. Mars gave its strength to both Aries and Scorpio, with the understanding that the Arian aspects were in ascendant while the Scorpion aspects were to be suppressed.

Elijah, the Scorpion

We should begin with those portions of Elijah's career that seem of a rather Scorpion nature.

21 Elijah went before the people and said, "How long will you waver between two opinions? If the LORD is God, follow him; but if Baal is God, follow him." But the people said nothing.

22 Then Elijah said to them, "I am the only one of the LORD's prophets left, but Baal has four hundred and fifty prophets.

23 Get two bulls for us. Let them choose one for themselves, and let them cut it into pieces and put it on the wood but not set fire to it. I will prepare the other bull and put it on the wood but not set fire to it.

24 Then you call on the name of your god, and I will call on the name of the LORD. The god who answers by fire--he is God." Then all the people said, "What you say is good."

25 Elijah said to the prophets of Baal, "Choose one of the bulls and prepare it first, since there are so many of you. Call on the name of your god, but do not light the fire."

26 So they took the bull given them and prepared it. Then they called on the name of Baal from morning till noon. "O Baal, answer us!" they shouted. But there was no response; no one answered. And they danced around the altar they had made.

27 At noon Elijah began to taunt them. "Shout louder!" he said. "Surely he is a god! Perhaps he is deep in thought, or busy, or traveling. Maybe he is sleeping and must be awakened."

28 So they shouted louder and slashed themselves with swords and spears, as was their custom, until their blood flowed.

29 Midday passed, and they continued their frantic prophesying until the time for the evening sacrifice. But there was no response, no one answered, no one paid attention.
(1Ki 18:21-29 NIV)

In our first example Elijah has set up a classic, my God is stronger than your god text.

30 Then Elijah said to all the people, "Come here to me." They came to him, and he repaired the altar of the LORD, which was in ruins.

31 Elijah took twelve stones, one for each of the tribes descended from Jacob, to whom the word of the LORD had come, saying, "Your name shall be Israel."

32 With the stones he built an altar in the name of the LORD, and he dug a trench around it large enough to hold two seahs of seed.

33 He arranged the wood, cut the bull into pieces and laid it on the wood. Then he said to them, "Fill four large jars with water and pour it on the offering and on the wood."

34 "Do it again," he said, and they did it again. "Do it a third time," he ordered, and they did it the third time.

35 The water ran down around the altar and even filled the trench.

36 At the time of sacrifice, the prophet Elijah stepped forward and prayed: "O LORD, God of Abraham, Isaac and Israel, let it be known today that you are God in Israel and that I am your servant and have done all these things at your command.

37 Answer me, O LORD, answer me, so these people will know that you, O LORD, are God, and that you are turning their hearts back again."

38 Then the fire of the LORD fell and burned up the sacrifice, the wood, the stones and the soil, and also licked up the water in the trench.

39 When all the people saw this, they fell prostrate and cried, "The LORD--he is God! The LORD--he is God!"

40 Then Elijah commanded them, "Seize the prophets of Baal. Don't let anyone get away!" They seized them, and Elijah had them brought down to the Kishon Valley and slaughtered there.

(1Ki 18:30-40 NIV)

Elijah's God wins by igniting the 'water.' But that is not enough, so Elijah also manages the slaughter of the four hundred and fifty prophets of Baal.

1 Some time later there was an incident involving a vineyard belonging to Naboth the Jezreelite. The vineyard was in Jezreel, close to the palace of Ahab king of Samaria.

2 Ahab said to Naboth, "Let me have your vineyard to use for a vegetable garden, since it is close to my palace. In exchange I will give you a better vineyard or, if you prefer, I will pay you whatever it is worth."

3 But Naboth replied, "The LORD forbid that I should give you the inheritance of my fathers."

4 So Ahab went home, sullen and angry because Naboth the Jezreelite had said, "I will not give you the inheritance of my fathers." He lay on his bed sulking and refused to eat.

5 His wife Jezebel came in and asked him, "Why are you so sullen? Why won't you eat?"

6 He answered her, "Because I said to Naboth the Jezreelite, 'Sell me your vineyard; or if you prefer, I will give you another vineyard in its place.' But he said, 'I will not give you my vineyard.'"

7 Jezebel his wife said, "Is this how you act as king over Israel? Get up and eat! Cheer up. I'll get you the vineyard of Naboth the Jezreelite."

8 So she wrote letters in Ahab's name, placed his seal on them, and sent them to the elders and nobles who lived in Naboth's city with him.

9 In those letters she wrote: "Proclaim a day of fasting and seat Naboth in a prominent place among the people.

10 But seat two scoundrels opposite him and have them testify that he has cursed both God and the king. Then take him out and stone him to death."

11 So the elders and nobles who lived in Naboth's city did as Jezebel directed in the letters she had written to them.

12 They proclaimed a fast and seated Naboth in a prominent place among the people.

13 Then two scoundrels came and sat opposite him and brought charges against Naboth before the people, saying, "Naboth has cursed both God and the king." So they took him outside the city and stoned him to death.

14 Then they sent word to Jezebel: "Naboth has been stoned and is dead."

15 As soon as Jezebel heard that Naboth had been stoned to death, she said to Ahab, "Get up and take possession of the vineyard of Naboth the Jezreelite that he refused to sell you. He is no longer alive, but dead."

16 When Ahab heard that Naboth was dead, he got up and went down to take possession of Naboth's vineyard.

17 Then the word of the LORD came to Elijah the Tishbite:

18 "Go down to meet Ahab king of Israel, who rules in Samaria. He is now in Naboth's vineyard, where he has gone to take possession of it.

19 Say to him, 'This is what the LORD says: Have you not murdered a man and seized his property?' Then say to him, 'This is what the LORD says: In the place where dogs licked up Naboth's blood, dogs will lick up your blood--yes, yours!' "

20 Ahab said to Elijah, "So you have found me, my enemy!" "I have found you," he answered, "because you have sold yourself to do evil in the eyes of the LORD.

21 'I am going to bring disaster on you. I will consume your descendants and cut off from Ahab every last male in Israel--slave or free.

22 I will make your house like that of Jeroboam son of Nebat and that of Baasha son of Ahijah, because you have provoked me to anger and have caused Israel to sin.'

23 "And also concerning Jezebel the LORD says: 'Dogs will devour Jezebel by the wall of Jezreel.'

24 "Dogs will eat those belonging to Ahab who die in the city, and the birds of the air will feed on those who die in the country."

25 (There was never a man like Ahab, who sold himself to do evil in the eyes of the LORD, urged on by Jezebel his wife.

26 He behaved in the vilest manner by going after idols, like the Amorites the LORD drove out before Israel.)

27 When Ahab heard these words, he tore his clothes, put on sackcloth and fasted. He lay in sackcloth and went around meekly.

28 Then the word of the LORD came to Elijah the Tishbite:

29 "Have you noticed how Ahab has humbled himself before me? Because he has humbled himself, I will not bring this disaster in his day, but I will bring it on his house in the days of his son."

(1Ki 21:1-29 NIV)

In the example above, Elijah responds to Ahab and Jezebel's actions by threatening that just as dogs licked up the blood of the innocent Naboth, so too will they feast on the bodies of Jezebel and Ahab. However, Elijah was not the best example of the Scorpion nature.

You will recall that earlier in this volume I presented the following verses as referring to John the Baptist:

9 "Which of you, if his son asks for bread, will give him a stone?
10 Or if he asks for a fish, will give him a snake?
(Mat 7:9-10 NIV)

I suggested that these verses refer to when the devil tempted Jesus to turn bread into stone, while the second half was a reference to John the Baptist who was supposed to be the fish of Pisces, but instead drowned Jesus and was, therefore, a snake. This verse has a second part which can be found in Luke:

11 Which of you fathers, if your son asks for a fish, will give him a snake instead?
12 Or if he asks for an egg, will give him a scorpion?
(Luk 11:11-12 NIV)

This time the verse begins with the son being given a snake instead of a fish, but then continues with the son being given, instead of an egg, a scorpion. The egg, in this instance, refers to the whole Jovian line of development from fish, to reptile, to bird. The son asks for an egg with the understanding that whatever he finds inside should come from one of those forms of life when instead he is given a scorpion, a form of life under the power of an entirely different god.

The Nazirite with the Gouged Out Eyes

Jesus said, "From Adam unto John the Baptist there has been none among the offspring of women who has been more exalted than John the Baptist, so that such a person's eyes might be destroyed. But I have said that whoever among you becomes a little one will become acquainted with the kingdom, and will become more exalted than John."
(GoT 46)

This saying is the only one within the Gospel of Thomas to explicitly mention John the Baptist. However, the bit about the eyes being destroyed has never been adequately explained. My understanding is that this is meant to connect John the Baptist to Samson, a hero with superhuman strength who was eventually taken captive and had his eyes gouged out by his enemies. Samson was a Nazirite:

2 A certain man of Zorah, named Manoah, from the clan of the Danites, had a wife who was sterile and remained childless.

3 The angel of the LORD appeared to her and said, "You are sterile and childless, but you are going to conceive and have a son.

4 Now see to it that you drink no wine or other fermented drink and that you do not eat anything unclean,

5 because you will conceive and give birth to a son. No razor may be used on his head, because the boy is to be a Nazirite, set apart to God from birth, and he will begin the deliverance of Israel from the hands of the Philistines."

(Jdg 13:2-5 NIV)

Compare the restrictions in common between Samson and John, the main difference being that nothing is said about John's hair.

13 But the angel said to him: "Do not be afraid, Zechariah; your prayer has been heard. Your wife Elizabeth will bear you a son, and you are to give him the name John.

14 He will be a joy and delight to you, and many will rejoice because of his birth,

15 for he will be great in the sight of the Lord. He is never to take wine or other fermented drink, and he will be filled with the Holy Spirit even from birth.

(Luk 1:13-15 NIV)

Let us now look at a few of Samson's adventures and see how they match up with both the Scorpion nature and with John the Baptist.

1 Samson went down to Timnah and saw there a young Philistine woman.

2 When he returned, he said to his father and mother, "I have seen a Philistine woman in Timnah; now get her for me as my wife."

3 His father and mother replied, "Isn't there an acceptable woman among your relatives or among all our people? Must you go to the uncircumcised Philistines to get a wife?" But Samson said to his father, "Get her for me. She's the right one for me."

4 (His parents did not know that this was from the LORD, who was seeking an occasion to confront the Philistines; for at that time they were ruling over Israel.)

5 Samson went down to Timnah together with his father and mother. As they approached the vineyards of Timnah, suddenly a young lion came roaring toward him.

6 The Spirit of the LORD came upon him in power so that he tore the lion apart with his bare hands as he might have torn a young goat. But he told neither his father nor his mother what he had done.

7 Then he went down and talked with the woman, and he liked her.

8 Some time later, when he went back to marry her, he turned aside to look at the lion's carcass. In it was a swarm of bees and some honey,

9 which he scooped out with his hands and ate as he went along. When he rejoined his parents, he gave them some, and they too ate it. But he did not tell them that he had taken the honey from the lion's carcass.

(Jdg 14:1-9 NIV)

Ok, we have Samson eating honey he found in the lion he killed.

4 John's clothes were made of camel's hair, and he had a leather belt around his waist. His food was locusts and wild honey.

(Mat 3:4 NIV)

Then, in Matthew above, we discover that wild honey made up a good portion of John's diet.

10 Now his father went down to see the woman. And Samson made a feast there, as was customary for bridegrooms.

11 When he appeared, he was given thirty companions.

12 "Let me tell you a riddle," Samson said to them. "If you can give me the answer within the seven days of the feast, I will give you thirty linen garments and thirty sets of clothes.

13 If you can't tell me the answer, you must give me thirty linen garments and thirty sets of clothes." "Tell us your riddle," they said. "Let's hear it."

14 He replied, "Out of the eater, something to eat; out of the strong, something sweet." For three days they could not give the answer.

15 On the fourth day, they said to Samson's wife, "Coax your husband into explaining the riddle for us, or we will burn you and your father's household to death. Did you invite us here to rob us?"

16 Then Samson's wife threw herself on him, sobbing, "You hate me! You don't really love me. You've given my people a riddle, but you haven't told me the answer." "I haven't even explained it to my father or mother," he replied, "so why should I explain it to you?"

17 She cried the whole seven days of the feast. So on the seventh day he finally told her, because she continued to press him. She in turn explained the riddle to her people.

18 Before sunset on the seventh day the men of the town said to him, "What is sweeter than honey? What is stronger than a lion?" Samson said to them, "If you had not plowed with my heifer, you would not have solved my riddle."

19 Then the Spirit of the LORD came upon him in power. He went down to Ashkelon, struck down thirty of their men, stripped them of their belongings and gave their clothes to those who had explained the riddle. Burning with anger, he went up to his father's house.

20 And Samson's wife was given to the friend who had attended him at his wedding.
(Jdg 14:10-1 NIV)

Notice that Samson's reactions are not exactly proportional to the injury or insult that he suffers.

1 Later on, at the time of wheat harvest, Samson took a young goat and went to visit his wife. He said, "I'm going to my wife's room." But her father would not let him go in.

2 "I was so sure you thoroughly hated her," he said, "that I gave her to your friend. Isn't her younger sister more attractive? Take her instead."

3 Samson said to them, "This time I have a right to get even with the Philistines; I will really harm them."

4 So he went out and caught three hundred foxes and tied them tail to tail in pairs. He then fastened a torch to every pair of tails,

5 lit the torches and let the foxes loose in the standing grain of the Philistines. He burned up the shocks and standing grain, together with the vineyards and olive groves.

6 When the Philistines asked, "Who did this?" they were told, "Samson, the Timnite's son-in-law, because his wife was given to his friend." So the Philistines went up and burned her and her father to death.

7 Samson said to them, "Since you've acted like this, I won't stop until I get my revenge on you."

8 He attacked them viciously and slaughtered many of them. Then he went down and stayed in a cave in the rock of Etam.

9 The Philistines went up and camped in Judah, spreading out near Lehi.

10 The men of Judah asked, "Why have you come to fight us?" "We have come to take Samson prisoner," they answered, "to do to him as he did to us."

11 Then three thousand men from Judah went down to the cave in the rock of Etam and said to Samson, "Don't you realize that the Philistines are rulers over us? What have you done to us?" He answered, "I merely did to them what they did to me."

12 They said to him, "We've come to tie you up and hand you over to the Philistines." Samson said, "Swear to me that you won't kill me yourselves."

13 "Agreed," they answered. "We will only tie you up and hand you over to them. We will not kill you." So they bound him with two new ropes and led him up from the rock.

14 As he approached Lehi, the Philistines came toward him shouting. The Spirit of the LORD came upon him in power. The ropes on his arms became like charred flax, and the bindings dropped from his hands.

15 Finding a fresh jawbone of a donkey, he grabbed it and struck down a thousand men.

16 Then Samson said, "With a donkey's jawbone I have made donkeys of them. With a donkey's jawbone I have killed a thousand men."

*17 When he finished speaking, he threw away the jawbone; and
the place was called Ramath Lehi.*

*18 Because he was very thirsty, he cried out to the LORD, "You
have given your servant this great victory. Must I now die of thirst
and fall into the hands of the uncircumcised?"*

*19 Then God opened up the hollow place in Lehi, and water
came out of it. When Samson drank, his strength returned and he
revived. So the spring was called En Hakkore, and it is still there in
Lehi.*

(Jdg 15:1-19 NIV)

Samson is the superhero who smashes and crushes and burns
and kills based solely on his wants and desires. He is not concerned
with the law or the nation of Israel. He is however very concerned
about his riddles and the secrecy surrounding their solutions:

*4 Some time later, he fell in love with a woman in the Valley of
Sorek whose name was Delilah.*

*5 The rulers of the Philistines went to her and said, "See if you
can lure him into showing you the secret of his great strength and
how we can overpower him so we may tie him up and subdue him.
Each one of us will give you eleven hundred shekels of silver."*

*6 So Delilah said to Samson, "Tell me the secret of your great
strength and how you can be tied up and subdued."*

*7 Samson answered her, "If anyone ties me with seven fresh
thongs that have not been dried, I'll become as weak as any other
man."*

*8 Then the rulers of the Philistines brought her seven fresh
thongs that had not been dried, and she tied him with them.*

*9 With men hidden in the room, she called to him, "Samson, the
Philistines are upon you!" But he snapped the thongs as easily as a
piece of string snaps when it comes close to a flame. So the secret of
his strength was not discovered.*

*10 Then Delilah said to Samson, "You have made a fool of me;
you lied to me. Come now, tell me how you can be tied."*

*11 He said, "If anyone ties me securely with new ropes that
have never been used, I'll become as weak as any other man."*

*12 So Delilah took new ropes and tied him with them. Then,
with men hidden in the room, she called to him, "Samson, the*

Philistines are upon you!" But he snapped the ropes off his arms as if they were threads.

13 Delilah then said to Samson, "Until now, you have been making a fool of me and lying to me. Tell me how you can be tied." He replied, "If you weave the seven braids of my head into the fabric on the loom and tighten it with the pin, I'll become as weak as any other man." So while he was sleeping, Delilah took the seven braids of his head, wove them into the fabric

14 and tightened it with the pin. Again she called to him, "Samson, the Philistines are upon you!" He awoke from his sleep and pulled up the pin and the loom, with the fabric.

15 Then she said to him, "How can you say, 'I love you,' when you won't confide in me? This is the third time you have made a fool of me and haven't told me the secret of your great strength."

16 With such nagging she prodded him day after day until he was tired to death.

17 So he told her everything. "No razor has ever been used on my head," he said, "because I have been a Nazirite set apart to God since birth. If my head were shaved, my strength would leave me, and I would become as weak as any other man."

18 When Delilah saw that he had told her everything, she sent word to the rulers of the Philistines, "Come back once more; he has told me everything." So the rulers of the Philistines returned with the silver in their hands.

19 Having put him to sleep on her lap, she called a man to shave off the seven braids of his hair, and so began to subdue him. And his strength left him.

20 Then she called, "Samson, the Philistines are upon you!" He awoke from his sleep and thought, "I'll go out as before and shake myself free." But he did not know that the LORD had left him.

21 Then the Philistines seized him, gouged out his eyes and took him down to Gaza. Binding him with bronze shackles, they set him to grinding in the prison.

(Jdg 16:4-21 NIV)

Samson is a more perfect representation of the Scorpion nature than Elijah. However Elijah was not described as dying within the Bible. Instead a chariot of fire appeared, and he was lifted up in a whirlwind. So it was assumed that Elijah would one day return, while Samson was explicitly declared as dead:

22 But the hair on his head began to grow again after it had been shaved.

23 Now the rulers of the Philistines assembled to offer a great sacrifice to Dagon their god and to celebrate, saying, "Our god has delivered Samson, our enemy, into our hands."

24 When the people saw him, they praised their god, saying, "Our god has delivered our enemy into our hands, the one who laid waste our land and multiplied our slain."

25 While they were in high spirits, they shouted, "Bring out Samson to entertain us." So they called Samson out of the prison, and he performed for them. When they stood him among the pillars,

26 Samson said to the servant who held his hand, "Put me where I can feel the pillars that support the temple, so that I may lean against them."

27 Now the temple was crowded with men and women; all the rulers of the Philistines were there, and on the roof were about three thousand men and women watching Samson perform.

28 Then Samson prayed to the LORD, "O Sovereign LORD, remember me. O God, please strengthen me just once more, and let me with one blow get revenge on the Philistines for my two eyes."

29 Then Samson reached toward the two central pillars on which the temple stood. Bracing himself against them, his right hand on the one and his left hand on the other,

30 Samson said, "Let me die with the Philistines!" Then he pushed with all his might, and down came the temple on the rulers and all the people in it. Thus he killed many more when he died than while he lived.

(Jdg 16:22-30 NIV)

John was more Samson reborn than Elijah, though he did gain the knowledge of breathing resuscitation from a study of Elijah and Elisha. Samson and John were both Nazirites, and they both met their downfall at the hands of women.

James, on the other hand, was Moses reborn, which basically meant he was concerned with preserving the law. Moses was on one side and Elijah/Samson on the other. Those aspects of life and the world that were aligned with Moses, with the law, were supported, were seen as positive, while those aspects that inspired soldiers or slaves to take matters into their own hands to extract their own personal vengeance, were suppressed. Mars gave its energy to both Aries and Scorpio, but it was Aries that grew in power as tribes grew into empires.

Pisces, the following age, had a different dynamic, that of fish versus bird. The philosophy of the fish was simple, to do to others as you would want them to do to you. This was to become especially important during longer sea voyages, where if a person fell overboard everyone would do whatever they could to save that person, including blowing air into their mouths or noses, whichever orifice was currently in vogue. The way of the bird, on the other hand, was that of the Will to Power, to reach one's goal regardless of the price.

John found himself in the role of the fish, while Jesus took the part of the bird and sacrificed his brother's genitals because he so loved his own.

We should now take another look at the brothers of Jesus together with the disciples to discover if there are any more cases of supposedly different individuals having the same name.

16 These are the twelve he appointed: Simon (to whom he gave the name Peter);

17 James son of Zebedee and his brother John (to them he gave the name Boanerges, which means Sons of Thunder);

18 Andrew, Philip, Bartholomew, Matthew, Thomas, James son of Alphaeus, Thaddaeus, Simon the Zealot

19 and Judas Iscariot, who betrayed him.
(Mar 3:16-19 NIV)

13 And when it was day he called his disciples, and having chosen out twelve from them, whom also he named apostles:

14 Simon, to whom also he gave the name of Peter, and Andrew his brother, and James and John, and Philip and Bartholomew,

15 and Matthew and Thomas, James the son of Alphaeus and Simon who was called Zealot,

16 and Judas brother of James, and Judas Iscariote, who was also his betrayer;
(Luk 6:13-16 DBY)

We really only need to examine the list of the apostles from Mark and Luke as there is no real difference between Mark and

Matthew. Luke has one difference, which is that the name of Thaddaeus has been replaced by Judas, brother of James.

So there are two Simons, which means that Simon Peter is the same as Simon the Zealot. There are also two apostles named James, so that means that James the son of Zebedee is the same as James, the son of Alphaeus.

Also, we know from the opening section of the Gospel of Thomas that Thomas the apostle was known as Didymus Judas Thomas. Both Didymus and Thomas mean twin, so what they were apparently going for was Judas Thomas the Twin. This means that there are three apostles named Judas: Judas, AKA Thaddaeus, brother of James, Judas Thomas and Judas Iscariot, which means they are one and the same.

Next, we will look at the list of brothers and once again we will only refer to the version from Mark:

3 Isn't this the carpenter? Isn't this Mary's son and the brother of James, Joseph, Judas and Simon? Aren't his sisters here with us?" And they took offense at him.
(Mar 6:3 NIV)

Brother Disciples

We see that in each case where there were two or more disciples with the same name there was also a brother with the same name: Simon, James, and Judas. There is also a brother named Joseph. This was the name of Jesus' supposed father, and by my rule, there should only be one person per name. If so, then as he was married to Mary and as Mary was Jesus's sister, he was Jesus's brother-in-law. Or perhaps, given that Mary's original husband was supposedly very old, he was assumed to have died, and this is his and Mary's son. Either way, he does not seem to be directly involved in Simon's machinations. He eventually returns to the story as Joseph of Arimathea. We have already examined James and Simon in some detail, but not so much Judas. What does it mean if Judas the brother of Jesus, Judas the brother of James, Judas Thomas and Judas Iscariot are the same person?

If Judas was just a reflection of Jesus, then Judas Iscariot's betrayal of Jesus was a reflection of Jesus' betrayal of John. Just as Judas Thomas' Gospel was a reflection of Jesus' hidden teachings.

I suspect that looking back with what I have now put together that the scene between Jesus and Salome had a deeper meaning:

Jesus said, Two will rest upon a couch; one will die, the other live.
Salome said, Who are you, man, whose son? You have mounted my couch and eaten from my table.
Jesus said to her, I am he who comes forth from the one who is integrated; I was given the things of my Father.
<Salome said,> I am your disciple.
<Jesus said to her,> Therefore I say, If he is integrated, he is full of light, but if he is divided, he will be full of darkness.
(GoT 61)

I believe that the two that rest upon a couch refers to Jesus and John. Jesus rests on her couch now, and John had done the same in the past. Looking at Samson's life, it is clear that the life of a Nazirite does not make one immune to the seductress. My impression is that Salome was initially destined to be married to John as Simon the angel solidified his control over both the masses and the current ruling dynasty. Salome was perhaps originally supposed to ask for the release of John the Baptist, which was all part of a plan concocted by Simon. But then Jesus came and convinced the goddess worshipers to take John out of the marriage market altogether.

Let us look for a moment at a scene between Jesus and the sons of Zebedee:

35 Then James and John, the sons of Zebedee, came to him. "Teacher," they said, "we want you to do for us whatever we ask."
36 "What do you want me to do for you?" he asked.
37 They replied, "Let one of us sit at your right and the other at your left in your glory."
38 "You don't know what you are asking," Jesus said. "Can you drink the cup I drink or be baptized with the baptism I am baptized with?"
39 "We can," they answered. Jesus said to them, "You will drink the cup I drink and be baptized with the baptism I am baptized with,

40 but to sit at my right or left is not for me to grant. These places belong to those for whom they have been prepared."
(Mar 10:35-40 NIV)

Matthew has the same story, but with one change. Matthew has added the character of Zebedee's wife to the scene. As you will recall, the Gospels dealt with the inconvenient presence of Salome in the narrative by making her the wife of Zebedee and therefore the mother of the sons of Zebedee. We, however, are privy to the information that the brothers each had a different mother, John's was Elizabeth and James' was Mary.

20 Then the mother of Zebedee's sons came to Jesus with her sons and, kneeling down, asked a favor of him.
21 "What is it you want?" he asked. She said, "Grant that one of these two sons of mine may sit at your right and the other at your left in your kingdom."
22 "You don't know what you are asking," Jesus said to them. "Can you drink the cup I am going to drink?" "We can," they answered.
23 Jesus said to them, "You will indeed drink from my cup, but to sit at my right or left is not for me to grant. These places belong to those for whom they have been prepared by my Father."
(Mat 20:20-23 NIV)

For now, let us consider their request as it concerns the wheel of the zodiac. In the previous age, Moses was on the left-hand side of the wheel symbolized by Aries and Elijah was on the right with Scorpio. Then in the age of Pisces, John was on the left as the fish and Jesus was on the right as the bird. This schema does not leave any room for James. However, in the creation account for the fifth day, which is ruled by the planet Jupiter, God creates fish, birds, and the great sea monsters:

21 And God created the great sea monsters, and every living soul that moves with which the waters swarm, after their kind, and every winged fowl after its kind. And God saw that it was good.
(Gen 1:21 DBY)

Basically, this left a middle ground for the life forms between fish and birds. The original word used is '*tannin*' which is translated as serpent, dragon, and sea monster. This allowed for the possibility of a trinity of sorts. If Jesus were to take the role of serpent or dragon, then there would be room for John on one side and James on the other. Jesus is shown shooting down the possibility. In Mark, he just says that those places are for those for whom they have been prepared. In Matthew, the text states that it is his father who determines who those seats are for. It could be argued that only one of the brothers got their wish, with John as the fish with his baptism but also his theology. On the right-hand side is Judas, the betrayer, the bird who acts to fulfill his will without concern for the cost. And between them, a serpent raised up on a pole.

6 And the LORD sent fiery serpents among the people, and they bit the people; and much people of Israel died.

7 Therefore the people came to Moses, and said, We have sinned, for we have spoken against the LORD, and against thee; pray unto the LORD, that he take away the serpents from us. And Moses prayed for the people.

8 And the LORD said unto Moses, Make thee a fiery serpent, and set it upon a pole: and it shall come to pass, that every one that is bitten, when he looketh upon it, shall live.

9 And Moses made a serpent of brass, and put it upon a pole, and it came to pass, that if a serpent had bitten any man, when he beheld the serpent of brass, he lived.
(Num 21:6-9 KJV)

This triad allowed for certain correspondences to develop. Those aspects of Christianity associated with John were seen as especially sacred. On the other hand, things related to Judas were seen as especially unholy. This was connected with the idea that the Judaeans, in general, were responsible for the betrayal and death of Jesus. So the gospel of John is the most sacred of the Gospels. The Synoptic Gospels are in the shadowy domain of Jesus on the cross, as are the texts contained in the Old Testament. You can study the stuff in the middle, but make sure that you do so from a Johannine perspective. And then there were the texts on the Judas side, the apocryphal and Gnostic texts, the possession of which was absolutely forbidden. But even here, those written in the Johannine tradition were considered the most sacred and they also supposedly provided the framework for the proper understanding the other gnostic texts. With the Revelation of John, the trilogy was complete as each domain was covered. The mysteries of the final book of the New Testament are to be found in the middle ground of the serpent on the cross. Not the safe world of John's Gospel, nor the forbidden realm of the secret book of John, but somewhere in between. A nice friendly Apocalypse with all the encrypted symbolism that implies along with a name you can trust. If it is called the Apocalypse of John, it must be good.

However, if such a triad existed, James lost out. This seems to be part of a repeating pattern. Elijah was the scorpion reborn as John, the fish. Judas Iscariot the bird is reborn as Judas Thomas the wise man. The old suppressed half is reborn as the new ascending force. James was Moses reborn but there no place in the new dynamic for Moses and his law. John and Judas ruled the age of Pisces. In the present dawning age, John's power will pass away while that of Judas will come to dominate in a new power dynamic between the forces of Aquarius and Capricorn.

Still, even with this triadic formation, the entire character of Judas in both forms is but a reflection of Jesus, as Judas is his twin. Judas serves as a dissociative identity entirely separate from Jesus. Jesus did not betray his brother, that guy was Judas Iscariot. Jesus did not create esoteric puzzles with surprising solutions, that guy was Judas Thomas.

Jesus and the Centurion

Returning to the story of Jesus and his brothers, the events surrounding the crucifixion take on a new significance. What was Jesus actually thinking was going to happen? First, we have to consider that Jesus was a man of two worlds. He was a Jew in Roman Palestine, and he was an initiate into the Mystery Religions at the highest level. He apparently had influence over at least one centurion officer.

5 When Jesus had entered Capernaum, a centurion came to him, asking for help.

6 "Lord," he said, "my servant lies at home paralyzed and in terrible suffering."

7 Jesus said to him, "I will go and heal him."

8 The centurion replied, "Lord, I do not deserve to have you come under my roof. But just say the word, and my servant will be healed.

9 For I myself am a man under authority, with soldiers under me. I tell this one, 'Go,' and he goes; and that one, 'Come,' and he comes. I say to my servant, 'Do this,' and he does it."

10 When Jesus heard this, he was astonished and said to those following him, "I tell you the truth, I have not found anyone in Israel with such great faith.

11 I say to you that many will come from the east and the west, and will take their places at the feast with Abraham, Isaac and Jacob in the Kingdom of Heaven.

12 But the subjects of the kingdom will be thrown outside, into the darkness, where there will be weeping and gnashing of teeth."

13 Then Jesus said to the centurion, "Go! It will be done just as you believed it would." And his servant was healed at that very hour.

(Mat 8:5-13 NIV)

Luke has the same story. Notice that while Matthew has a dig against the Jews, Luke has Jewish elders serving as messengers for the centurion:

2 There a centurion's servant, whom his master valued highly, was sick and about to die.

3 The centurion heard of Jesus and sent some elders of the Jews to him, asking him to come and heal his servant.

4 When they came to Jesus, they pleaded earnestly with him, "This man deserves to have you do this,

5 because he loves our nation and has built our synagogue."

6 So Jesus went with them. He was not far from the house when the centurion sent friends to say to him: "Lord, don't trouble yourself, for I do not deserve to have you come under my roof.

7 That is why I did not even consider myself worthy to come to you. But say the word, and my servant will be healed.

8 For I myself am a man under authority, with soldiers under me. I tell this one, 'Go,' and he goes; and that one, 'Come,' and he comes. I say to my servant, 'Do this,' and he does it."

9 When Jesus heard this, he was amazed at him, and turning to the crowd following him, he said, "I tell you, I have not found such great faith even in Israel."
10 Then the men who had been sent returned to the house and found the servant well.
(Luk 7:2-10 NIV)

In Luke's version, the Jewish elders are happy to assist the centurion in his attempt to contact Jesus because the Roman officer had built their synagogue. Perhaps this Roman officer might be willing to turn a blind eye to a rescue attempt of a crucifixion victim. What I am suggesting is that Jesus expected he was going to be removed from the crucifix and another body put in his place. So they needed an inside man among the Roman troops guarding the field of crucifixion. Not that Jesus had any reason to really worry. If things got out of hand, he knew that his father could muster up an army of bloodthirsty zealots, many of whom were among the five thousand fed by the five loaves.

53 Do you think I cannot call on my Father, and he will at once put at my disposal more than twelve legions of angels?
(Mat 26:53 NIV)

Let us now examine the events around the crucifixion to see how our new understanding changes their significance.

21 A certain man from Cyrene, Simon, the father of Alexander and Rufus, was passing by on his way in from the country, and they forced him to carry the cross.
22 They brought Jesus to the place called Golgotha (which means The Place of the Skull).
23 Then they offered him wine mixed with myrrh, but he did not take it.
24 And they crucified him. Dividing up his clothes, they cast lots to see what each would get.
25 It was the third hour when they crucified him.
26 The written notice of the charge against him read: THE KING OF THE JEWS.
27 They crucified two robbers with him, one on his right and one on his left.

(Mar 15:21-27 NIV)

Simon the Cyrene

In Mark's version, Simon the Cyrene is described as the father of Alexander and Rufus.

Given that we know that this Simon is the same as all the others we can assume that the name of his sons has some correlation to the sons of Zebedee, James and John. The name Rufus means red. Alexander means protector of man. Alexander is, of course, the name of the ruler Alexander the Great. Assuming that the order of the names remains unchanged from one Simon to another, James corresponds to Alexander and John to Rufus. This means that James was associated with empire while John was associated with the color red. This matches up with Elizabeth weaving the red when Mary comes to visit while being pregnant with Jesus. Basically this translates as James being a supporter of laws, while John was more concerned with violence and the spilling of blood.

32 As they were going out, they met a man from Cyrene, named Simon, and they forced him to carry the cross.

33 They came to a place called Golgotha (which means The Place of the Skull).

34 There they offered Jesus wine to drink, mixed with gall; but after tasting it, he refused to drink it.

35 When they had crucified him, they divided up his clothes by casting lots.

36 And sitting down, they kept watch over him there.

37 Above his head they placed the written charge against him: THIS IS JESUS, THE KING OF THE JEWS.

38 Two robbers were crucified with him, one on his right and one on his left.

(Mat 27:32-38 NIV)

Matthew follows Mark reasonably closely, though with Jesus sampling the gall before refusing it. Also, it seems clear that the two thieves crucified to his left and right are supposed to remind the reader of James and John asking to sit at the left and right of Jesus in his glory.

26 As they led him away, they seized Simon from Cyrene, who was on his way in from the country, and put the cross on him and made him carry it behind Jesus.

27 A large number of people followed him, including women who mourned and wailed for him.

28 Jesus turned and said to them, "Daughters of Jerusalem, do not weep for me; weep for yourselves and for your children.

29 For the time will come when you will say, 'Blessed are the barren women, the wombs that never bore and the breasts that never nursed!'

30 Then " 'they will say to the mountains, "Fall on us!" and to the hills, "Cover us!" '

31 For if men do these things when the tree is green, what will happen when it is dry?"

32 Two other men, both criminals, were also led out with him to be executed.

33 When they came to the place called the Skull, there they crucified him, along with the criminals--one on his right, the other on his left.

34 Jesus said, "Father, forgive them, for they do not know what they are doing." And they divided up his clothes by casting lots.

(Luk 23:26-34 NIV)

In Luke above, Jesus reminds everyone that the end times are not happy times for pregnant mothers. Then we have Jesus directing a line to his father so we can take that as meaning that Simon is still with him.

29 Those who passed by hurled insults at him, shaking their heads and saying, "So! You who are going to destroy the temple and build it in three days,

30 come down from the cross and save yourself!"

31 In the same way the chief priests and the teachers of the law mocked him among themselves. "He saved others," they said, "but he can't save himself!

32 Let this Christ, this King of Israel, come down now from the cross, that we may see and believe." Those crucified with him also heaped insults on him.

33 At the sixth hour darkness came over the whole land until the ninth hour.

(Mar 15:29-33 NIV)

In Mark, the insults focus on Jesus' inability to save himself.

39 Those who passed by hurled insults at him, shaking their heads
40 and saying, "You who are going to destroy the temple and build it in three days, save yourself! Come down from the cross, if you are the Son of God!"
41 In the same way the chief priests, the teachers of the law and the elders mocked him.
42 "He saved others," they said, "but he can't save himself! He's the King of Israel! Let him come down now from the cross, and we will believe in him.
43 He trusts in God. Let God rescue him now if he wants him, for he said, 'I am the Son of God.' "
44 In the same way the robbers who were crucified with him also heaped insults on him.
45 From the sixth hour until the ninth hour darkness came over all the land.
(Mat 27:39-45 NIV)

Matthew begins with insults focusing on Jesus' inability to save himself, but then they turn to God and how God should rescue him if he is, in fact, the son of God.

35 The people stood watching, and the rulers even sneered at him. They said, "He saved others; let him save himself if he is the Christ of God, the Chosen One."
36 The soldiers also came up and mocked him. They offered him wine vinegar
37 and said, "If you are the king of the Jews, save yourself."
38 There was a written notice above him, which read: THIS IS THE KING OF THE JEWS.
39 One of the criminals who hung there hurled insults at him: "Aren't you the Christ? Save yourself and us!"
40 But the other criminal rebuked him. "Don't you fear God," he said, "since you are under the same sentence?
41 We are punished justly, for we are getting what our deeds deserve. But this man has done nothing wrong."

42 Then he said, "Jesus, remember me when you come into your kingdom. "

43 Jesus answered him, "I tell you the truth, today you will be with me in paradise. "

(Luk 23:35-43 NIV)

In Mark, the insults were identified as coming from three groups: people passing by, the chief priests and the teachers of the law, and those crucified with him. Matthew also mentions those three groups. Mark and Matthew both give examples of the sort of comments coming from the first two groups. Luke moves from insults by people passing by and the Jewish priest and elders to the remarks made by the two thieves themselves.

My God, Why?

34 And at the ninth hour Jesus cried out in a loud voice, "Eloi, Eloi, lama sabachthani?"--which means, "My God, my God, why have you forsaken me?"

35 When some of those standing near heard this, they said, "Listen, he's calling Elijah. "

36 One man ran, filled a sponge with wine vinegar, put it on a stick, and offered it to Jesus to drink. "Now leave him alone. Let's see if Elijah comes to take him down," he said.

37 With a loud cry, Jesus breathed his last.

38 The curtain of the temple was torn in two from top to bottom.

39 And when the centurion, who stood there in front of Jesus, heard his cry and saw how he died, he said, "Surely this man was the Son of God!"

(Mar 15:34-39 NIV)

The section from Mark above has two crucial features. The first is Jesus calling out to Eloi, which is the singular of Elohim. This is Jesus calling out to his father, the archangel Gabriel, who is one of the Elohim. The other notable feature is the centurion standing at the feet of Jesus. My view is that this centurion was there, waiting for the followers of Jesus to come and him, and putting a body upon the cross in his place. He remained until Jesus died.

46 About the ninth hour Jesus cried out in a loud voice, "Eloi, Eloi, lama sabachthani?"--which means, "My God, my God, why have you forsaken me?"

47 When some of those standing there heard this, they said, "He's calling Elijah."

48 Immediately one of them ran and got a sponge. He filled it with wine vinegar, put it on a stick, and offered it to Jesus to drink.

49 The rest said, "Now leave him alone. Let's see if Elijah comes to save him."

50 And when Jesus had cried out again in a loud voice, he gave up his spirit.

51 At that moment the curtain of the temple was torn in two from top to bottom. The earth shook and the rocks split.

52 The tombs broke open and the bodies of many holy people who had died were raised to life.

53 They came out of the tombs, and after Jesus' resurrection they went into the holy city and appeared to many people.

54 When the centurion and those with him who were guarding Jesus saw the earthquake and all that had happened, they were terrified, and exclaimed, "Surely he was the Son of God!"

(Mat 27:46-54 NIV)

Matthew makes everything apocalyptic, with the tombs being broken open and the people being brought back to life. This seems to be done all so that the centurion would have a reason for declaring Jesus the son of God. This leads me to believe that the centurion's words in Mark were actually meant to convey the idea that the centurion was confirming to himself that he was in the right place, that his man being crucified before him was without a doubt, the son of God. And so he was left wondering what had happened with the whole rescue plan.

44 It was now about the sixth hour, and darkness came over the whole land until the ninth hour,

45 for the sun stopped shining. And the curtain of the temple was torn in two.

46 Jesus called out with a loud voice, "Father, into your hands I commit my spirit." When he had said this, he breathed his last.

47 The centurion, seeing what had happened, praised God and said, "Surely this was a righteous man."

(Luk 23:44-47 NIV)

Luke goes for a simplified version. Here Jesus speaks directly to his father, indicating that Simon was still within earshot. The centurion's comment is one that reflects his feelings of loss and frustration that he had not been given the agreed upon signal. Apparently, the signal was supposed to come from Simon, but it was never given.

Perhaps Simon explained to Jesus while he was suffering on the cross why there would be no rescue. Jesus was the bird who had betrayed his brother, and by doing so also betrayed his father by ruining his father's plans. Jesus was the purest of pure, his father's favorite son. He was the bird, exercising his will to power and his brother was the fish, left sexless by Jesus' betrayal. The law of the astrological ages stipulated even though Jupiter gave its strength to both Pisces and Sagittarius equally, inevitably the fish must thrive, and the bird must fall. The fish represented the poor ignorant masses, while the bird represented the wealthy elite. The logic of the ages dictated that, after an astrological age, the fish would eventually triumph over the bird after which the whole system would be reorganized in accordance with an entirely new dynamic.

Are You the One?

There are a few loose ends I should tie down. Concerning John the Baptist, during the time he was imprisoned, he supposedly sent some of his followers to find Jesus and interview him:

2 When John heard in prison what Christ was doing, he sent his disciples

3 to ask him, "Are you the one who was to come, or should we expect someone else?"

4 Jesus replied, "Go back and report to John what you hear and see:

5 The blind receive sight, the lame walk, those who have leprosy are cured, the deaf hear, the dead are raised, and the good news is preached to the poor.

6 Blessed is the man who does not fall away on account of me."
(Mat 11:2-6 NIV)

17 This news about Jesus spread throughout Judea and the surrounding country.

18 John's disciples told him about all these things. Calling two of them,

19 he sent them to the Lord to ask, "Are you the one who was to come, or should we expect someone else?"

20 When the men came to Jesus, they said, "John the Baptist sent us to you to ask, 'Are you the one who was to come, or should we expect someone else?'"

21 At that very time Jesus cured many who had diseases, sicknesses and evil spirits, and gave sight to many who were blind.

22 So he replied to the messengers, "Go back and report to John what you have seen and heard: The blind receive sight, the lame walk, those who have leprosy are cured, the deaf hear, the dead are raised, and the good news is preached to the poor.

23 Blessed is the man who does not fall away on account of me."

(Luk 7:17-23 NIV)

In both Matthew and Luke, we have Jesus being interviewed by either some or two of John's followers. They ask if Jesus is the one. Jesus answers that he has done all of the things on the checklist from Isaiah. If such an event occurred, it would have to have taken place after John baptized Jesus but before Jesus met up with John and James, the sons of Zebedee, according to my theory that John the Baptist is identical to John, son of Zebedee. My position is that the timeline of John the Baptist has been shifted within the Gospels to hide the relationship between the two Johns. As I see it, John baptized Jesus. Jesus and Simon then retreated to the desert. Jesus hung out with Simon and the two groups, as the women following Jesus and the men who had been following John but were now following Simon, merged. Jesus proceeded to work miracles when John contacted him from prison. I suspect that his message was meant as a reminder.

"Well, if you are finally ready to play the role our father has prepared for you, then tell him to take the necessary steps to get me released."

As you may recall, I previously put forth the possibility that Simon had arranged for John to marry Salome in an attempt to cement Simon's influence over the opposing factions. This is obviously pure speculation a level beyond my usual layer of informed speculation. Still, I like to believe that John was signaling to Jesus not to forget about him rotting in a dungeon, and no hard feelings about the drowning, right, Brother?

The message however likely pushed Jesus to get John fixed as soon as possible. If John had heard of Jesus' activities inside prison, then any informers of the goddess would likely know that Jesus had yet to be redeemed.

Simon, Son of John

In Mark and Matthew, Jesus first meets the disciples Simon and Andrew, and then John and James while walking by the sea. Luke however never really shows when Jesus met Simon, which makes sense if Simon had been with him since the baptism, accompanying him through the desert and traveling with him as he goes from place to place, working miracles. This reordering of events allows for word of Jesus and his miracles to reach John in prison before Jesus ever meets the sons of Zebedee.

Then there are the events described in the gospel of John. I generally refrain from citing the gospel of John because it is a dangerous text. It seems to be providing a window through which a new level of knowledge is being offered, but the knowledge is tainted and twisted. Still, we can see that in John's gospel, Andrew is identified as a disciple of John the Baptist, who, after encountering Jesus, brings Simon to meet him:

28 This all happened at Bethany on the other side of the Jordan, where John was baptizing.

29 The next day John saw Jesus coming toward him and said, "Look, the Lamb of God, who takes away the sin of the world!

30 This is the one I meant when I said, 'A man who comes after me has surpassed me because he was before me.'

31 I myself did not know him, but the reason I came baptizing with water was that he might be revealed to Israel."

32 Then John gave this testimony: "I saw the Spirit come down from heaven as a dove and remain on him.

33 I would not have known him, except that the one who sent me to baptize with water told me, 'The man on whom you see the

Spirit come down and remain is he who will baptize with the Holy Spirit.'

34 I have seen and I testify that this is the Son of God."

35 The next day John was there again with two of his disciples.

36 When he saw Jesus passing by, he said, "Look, the Lamb of God!"

37 When the two disciples heard him say this, they followed Jesus.

38 Turning around, Jesus saw them following and asked, "What do you want?" They said, "Rabbi" (which means Teacher), "where are you staying?"

39 "Come," he replied, "and you will see." So they went and saw where he was staying, and spent that day with him. It was about the tenth hour.

40 Andrew, Simon Peter's brother, was one of the two who heard what John had said and who had followed Jesus.

41 The first thing Andrew did was to find his brother Simon and tell him, "We have found the Messiah" (that is, the Christ).

42 And he brought him to Jesus. Jesus looked at him and said, "You are Simon son of John. You will be called Cephas" (which, when translated, is Peter).

(Joh 1:28-42 NIV)

John's gospel takes it as a given that John the Baptist knew Simon and the guys. This gospel gives a lot of support to the theory, until, in the end, Jesus calls Simon the son of John. Of course, according to our theory, Simon has no human parents.

Jesus said: When you see him who was not born of woman, fall down upon your faces and worship him; that one is your Father.
(GoT 15)

Simon, Son of Jonah

13 When Jesus came to the region of Caesarea Philippi, he asked his disciples, "Who do people say the Son of Man is?"

14 They replied, "Some say John the Baptist; others say Elijah; and still others, Jeremiah or one of the prophets."

15 "But what about you?" he asked. "Who do you say I am?"

16 Simon Peter answered, "You are the Christ, the Son of the living God."

17 Jesus replied, "Blessed are you, Simon son of Jonah, for this was not revealed to you by man, but by my Father in heaven.

18 And I tell you that you are Peter, and on this rock I will build my church, and the gates of Hades will not overcome it.

19 I will give you the keys of the kingdom of heaven; whatever you bind on earth will be bound in heaven, and whatever you loose on earth will be loosed in heaven."

(Mat 16:13-19 NIV)

In the section from Matthew above, Jesus asks the disciples who they think he is. Simon answers that Jesus is the Christ, the Son of the living God. Jesus seems pleased, and he calls Simon by his patronym Simon son of Jonah. But suppose Jesus, in fact, is not happy. Let us suppose that this idea of being the Son of God was not something that Jesus had agreed to or more importantly, it was not something that he agreed to have announced. But here comes Simon, blurting it out and so Jesus says that Simon is the son of Jonah, which Jesus is using as short-hand for a fisherman, though to be honest the prophet Jonah was more bait than fisherman as it was the fish that caught him.

Nonetheless, Jesus is telling Simon that his disguise as a simple fisherman is blown and Jesus is no longer going to allow him to influence things from the shadows. He drags him into the light, and then he drops his church on him, a church which the gates of hell will not overcome. He presses his church down on Simon, someone who he regularly calls Satan, and he essentially says that the gates of hell leading to this church will never be opened. But the gates of heaven leading to and from this church will be opened and whatever is loosed or bound in one will be loosed or bound in the other.

What Jesus seems to be saying to Simon is that fine, go ahead and make whatever announcements you want but be aware that when you do, the things you are announcing are being locked down in stone. If Simon has a direct line to the living God then whatever Simon says will be considered to have been dictated by God.

Naturally, the very next thing out of Simon Peter's mouth is a refutation of Jesus' plan.

21 From that time on Jesus began to explain to his disciples that he must go to Jerusalem and suffer many things at the hands of the elders, chief priests and teachers of the law, and that he must be killed and on the third day be raised to life.

22 Peter took him aside and began to rebuke him. "Never, Lord!" he said. "This shall never happen to you!"

23 Jesus turned and said to Peter, "Get behind me, Satan! You are a stumbling block to me; you do not have in mind the things of God, but the things of men."

(Mat 16:21-23 NIV)

Jesus claims that Peter does not have in mind the things of God, but rather the things of man. Yet three verses earlier Jesus declared that whatever Peter loosed on earth he also loosed in heaven. Peter and God spoke with the same voice. Still, when he told Jesus that the events Jesus described would never happen, it seems he really only took issue with the final event on the list, where on the third day Jesus is raised to life. That was what he meant when he said, "Never, Lord! This shall never happen to you!"

Mary's House: Clean and Orderly No More

Concerning Mary, earlier I wrote about Mary, who was the mother, sister, and lover of Jesus and how he had saved her from seven evil spirits, which I have interpreted as rescuing Mary from a household of children bred from both the angel Gabriel and men of the seven pure bloodlines. After many years learning the secrets of the goddess, Jesus returned with Mary by his side. He found a safe place for her to stay and he went and met John and his baptism. Then he retreated to the desert with his father.

24 "When an evil spirit comes out of a man, it goes through arid places seeking rest and does not find it. Then it says, 'I will return to the house I left.'

25 When it arrives, it finds the house swept clean and put in order.

26 Then it goes and takes seven other spirits more wicked than itself, and they go in and live there. And the final condition of that man is worse than the first."

27 As Jesus was saying these things, a woman in the crowd called out, "Blessed is the mother who gave you birth and nursed you."
(Luk 11:24-27 NIV)

In the parable above, Jesus is the evil spirit that has come out of Mary. Jesus has left her; she is safe in her home. Jesus encounters John and then goes into the desert with his father.

Eventually, after John is castrated and Mary asks Jesus to treat his injury, Jesus and Mary reunite, while the rest of his brothers, Simon, and assorted followers move in and make themselves at home. This is what happens when the evil spirit returns to the person it had possessed and finds the house clean and in order. Then seven spirits more wicked than the first move in. Now Mary's house is once again a real mess.

<u>Conclusion</u>

And so the hidden mythos is revealed. Jesus was the grandson and son of the archangel Gabriel, who took part in and then hijacked a secret breeding project being conducted by the followers of the goddess.

Jesus rescued Mary from the clutches of this angel, and they disappeared among the followers of the goddess who then taught Jesus the secrets that no man could lawfully know. Jesus was obligated to undergo castration after learning these secrets, but an arrangement was made whereby Jesus could substitute a suitable sacrifice in place of his own.

Meanwhile, Simon had been using John and the other male siblings of Jesus to build a following. John was baptizing initiates, which involved actual drowning and resuscitation. The group was likely moving up the river Jordan in fishing boats from which Simon and his boys performed various miraculous feats ending in a baptism. The baptism was probably usually done on a shill hidden in the audience, but sometimes, if someone new wanted to join the group, they might get the full works.

Once word spread about the baptisms they may have had to provide both real baptisms where people actually drowned and then resuscitated as well as purely ritual baptisms for when the authorities were watching.

Then Jesus shows up, and John recognizes him as Simon's favorite son returned at last. He is the bird to John's fish. However, Jesus refuses to baptize John but instead submits to baptism by John, which means that Jesus is posing as a fish while concealing his true nature. John drowns Jesus, after which Simon dives into the Jordan and rescues him.

Jesus and Simon retreat to the desert where Simon tries to convince Jesus to go along with his plans, while Jesus has his own program based on an esoteric reinterpretation of certain parts of the Old Testament.

Simon's plans included using marrying John to Salome while using Jesus to unify the mystery religions as the high priest(ess) with his consort Mary by his side. Notice that none of the temptations used by the devil involve Jesus leaving descendants. That was already off the table.

Jesus planned the events leading up to his death and the aftermath as pieces of a ritual sacrifice that would override once and for all the need to repeatedly slaughter animals as sacrifices to God.

However, he was not planning on actually dying. Basically, Jesus together with his father and brothers were magicians. They were both stage magicians and ritual magicians.

31 He then began to teach them that the Son of Man must suffer many things and be rejected by the elders, chief priests and teachers of the law, and that he must be killed and after three days rise again. (Mar 8:31 NIV)

The verse above, where Jesus reveals all that will befall him, is the same sort of spiel a magician uses to rile up the audience. It was all part of his plan, except he would only be on the cross until darkness fell when he could be replaced on the cross by a carefully chosen corpse. Perhaps he planned to use Judas's body. Considering that we are dealing with stage magicians, I suspect Judas Thomas the Twin was given that moniker because of his ability to impersonate others, not just Jesus. Even so, I think Jesus planned for the lifeless body of Judas to take his place on the cross. After all, Judas did betray him, even if that betrayal was all scripted and prearranged

Then Jesus was to hide himself away in the tomb of Joseph of Arimathea along with the corpse from the cross for three days, after which he would arise and enjoy the rest of his life with Mary by his side and genitals firmly in place, worshipped by Jews, Greeks and Romans as the sacred Son of the Lord God.

An essential part of his plan was to have someone else's genitals on the chopping block. That someone turned out to be John the Baptist. Jesus hooked up with Salome at Herod's birthday party, and he convinced her to ask for John's manhood on a platter rather than asking that John be set free (so that they might later marry).

John gets castrated. He is then released to his family and followers. Mary sends a message to Jesus to come and treat John from his emasculation. Jesus complies, using the techniques he learned from his time spent among the followers of the goddess.

With John healed, the gang is back together, this time with Jesus as the leader while the angel Gabriel pulls strings from the shadows disguised as a legion of different men named Simon.

Granted, much of what I have written is not found concealed within the Gospels, such as Simon planning for John to marry Salome or the actual plan Jesus had organized so that he might avoid dying on the cross. I am attempting to extrapolate from the scanty information supplied.

Still, I would be doing the reader a grave disservice if I gave the impression that I take any of this as actually something which actually occurred in the past. My position is that these texts are encrypted literary works and should not be confused as being records of events which actually happened.

The current tendency in Biblical criticism is to search for the historical kernel. This involves finding the earliest uncorrupted recorded stories or sayings of Jesus. This basically reduces our knowledge to what is found in Mark and the supposed text of Q. This view ignores much of Luke and Matthew as being nothing more than a reproduction of what is found in Mark together with an elaboration of the original text.

Mark sets down the original story, and Matthew takes that story and adds some details and twists it one way, while Luke, independently of Matthew, takes the same story, adds different features, and twists it another way. According to the critical view, both Mathew and Luke's versions can be ignored as Mark is the earliest version which is, therefore, closer to the historical Jesus.

I, however, am not interested in the historical Jesus. I am also not interested in the Jesus of Christian theology. My interest is in the Jesus whose teaching has been hidden and encrypted within the Synoptic Gospels and the works of Thomasine Gnosticism.

Returning to the chart that I included at the beginning of this volume:

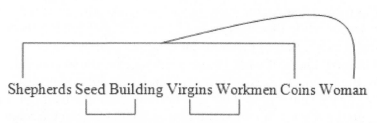

Figure 14. Pairs among the seven parables.

We can now better appreciate the structure created by the ordering of the seven parables. The parables indicated by the titles of Shepherds and Coins are two members of the three parable set concluding with The Prodigal Son. In my version of The Prodigal Son story, when the youngest son returns, his father puts on a big celebration at which the son is sacrificed. This story is paired with the parable of The Woman.

The parable of The Woman keeps unwinding further and further, beginning with the Kingdom of Heaven sayings and then the Kingdom of the Father sayings, to gender switching and ritual castration, to the mothers of the genealogies and the eight bloodlines. Eventually, an angel joins the dance, and it becomes the woman and the angel, a combination which is often a precursor to unpleasant events.

Things then begin to form patterns. Jesus becomes the Prodigal Son, who flees with his inheritance, his Mary. He goes to a distant land, where he spends his time with the sacred prostitutes. Eventually, he returns to his father and older brother. His father arranges a big event for him which ends in his sacrifice. Now we see that behind it all is the ritual castration required by the cult of the goddess and Jesus being unwilling to pay the price with his own flesh. This results in Jesus betraying his older brother John, which throws a wrench into their father's big plans.

From my reading, the father always knows that the younger son is going to end up castrated. He has already written him off when the younger son runs off to live with the prostitutes. Then Jesus returns with all pieces attached, and his father realizes that the goddess is once again interfering with Father's work.

This is not to suggest that the angel does not deserve most of the blame for hijacking the breeding project and staying around after his one-time breeding duty is completed by his successful impregnation

188

of Anna. The next generation's breeding partner was supposed to be from the bloodline of Joseph according to the genealogy, but the angel inserts himself into the final stage of the project by impregnating his own daughter and fathering a son named Jesus.

These various interpersonal relationships make up the hidden mythos. While this is also a part of the secret teachings, it is on a different level than the basic understanding of the spheres as revealed in the parables labeled The Seed and The Building. An even more profound understanding of the spheres together with astrology is needed to understand the inner meanings of the parables labeled The Virgins and The Workmen.

One has to admire how the various parables are nested in pairs with The Woman as the final piece in the series. This has to be the last piece to be solved because doing so flips the signifiers, one after another, like parallel rows of toppling dominoes, until the meaning of everything has been transformed.

List of Figures

<u>Works Cited</u>

I use a variety of different Biblical translations. My order of preference is the *Darby Bible* from 1884-1890, which is basically a literal translation. If that translation uses too strange terms I then go to the *King James Version* from 1611-1769. If that is too difficult to parse I try the *New English Translation* from 2005, though the editors may be a bit too creative. When I want an understandable version in modern English I use the *New International Version* 1984. For those times when I want a literal translation and Darby is not adequate, I might turn to *Young's Literal Translation* from 1862-1898. When all else fails I try the *Complete Jewish Bible* from 1998.

The verses from the *Gospel of Thomas* are my own translation that is based on a comparison of translations by Stephen Patterson and Marvin Meyer, Thomas O. Lambdin, Marvin Meyer, Stevan Davies and Michael W. Grondin's Interlinear Translation.

Bailey, C. (1921). *Lucretius on the nature of things.* Clarendon Press.
Burton, R. (1928). *The Carmina of Caius Valerius Catullus.* Privately Printed.
Charles, R. (1917). *The Book of Enoch.* Society for Promoting Christian Knowledge.
Dryden, J. (1751). *Ovid's Metamorphoses.* London.
Isenberg, W. W. (1988). *The Nag Hammadi Library in English.* Harper San Francisco.
James, M. (1924). *Gospel of James, OR Protoevangelium of James.* Oxford: Clarendon Press.
Kline, A. S. (2013). *Lucius Apuleius The Golden Ass.*
Oldfather. (1933). *Diodorus of Sicily: the library of history.* Harvard University Press.
Polišenský, M. (1991). *The language and Origin of the Etruscans.* Transal Books.
Strong, H. A. (1913). *The Syrian Goddess by Lucian.* London.
Turner, J. D. (n.d.). *The Book of Thomas the Contender.*
Vermes, G. (n.d.). *The Complete Dead Sea Scrolls in English.* 1997: The Penguin Press.

<u>Bibliography</u>

Schonfield, H. (1965). *The Passover Plot.* Hutchinson.

Before You Go

From the Author: Reviews are gold to authors! If you've enjoyed this book, would you consider Writing a Review?

If you did not enjoy the book or had a problem with it, please contact me at lambert.timothy.j@gmail.com

Would you like to know when my next book is available? You can follow me on Twitter @gnosty

Made in the USA
Coppell, TX
28 November 2020

42331302R00121